THE OPPOSITIONAL DEFIANT DISORDER GUIDE

TACKLE DAILY DISRUPTIONS, ADDRESS CONSTANT DEFIANCE AND PARENT BURNOUT, ENHANCE COMMUNICATION, AND ACHIEVE STRONGER BONDS FOR A TRANQUIL HOME

MICHAEL KARL

© **Copyright Michael Karl 2024 - All rights reserved.**

The content within this book may not be reproduced, duplicated or transmitted without direct written permission from the author or the publisher.

Under no circumstances will any blame or legal responsibility be held against the publisher, or author, for any damages, reparation, or monetary loss due to the information contained within this book. Either directly or indirectly. You are responsible for your own choices, actions, and results.

Legal Notice:

This book is copyright protected. This book is only for personal use. You cannot amend, distribute, sell, use, quote or paraphrase any part, of the content within this book, without the consent of the author or publisher.

Disclaimer Notice:

Please note the information contained within this document is for educational and entertainment purposes only. All effort has been expended to present accurate, up-to-date, and reliable, complete information. No warranties of any kind are declared or implied. Readers acknowledge that the author is not engaging in the rendering of legal, financial, medical or professional advice. The content within this book has been derived from various sources. Please consult a licensed professional before attempting any techniques outlined in this book.

By reading this document, the reader agrees that under no circumstances is the author responsible for any losses, direct or indirect, which are incurred as a result of the use of the information contained within this document, including, but not limited to, — errors, omissions, or inaccuracies.

CONTENTS

Introduction ... 7

1. **UNDERSTANDING ODD, ITS SYMPTOMS, AND HOW IT DIFFERS FROM OTHER BEHAVIORAL DISORDERS** ... 11
   Decoding the Symptoms of ODD: Beyond Defiance ... 12
   How ODD Differs from Other Behavioral Disorders and Common Coexisting Conditions ... 13
   Understanding Overlap and Interplay Between Disorders ... 17
   Understanding the Biological Basis of ODD ... 17
   Recognizing and Understanding the Early Signs and Progression of Oppositional Defiant Disorder ... 20
   Case Study: Navigating Life with a Child Diagnosed with ODD ... 23
   Observation and Documentation Process ... 25
   The Misconceptions of ODD: Debunking Harmful Myths ... 29

2. **STRENGTHENING FAMILY RELATIONSHIPS WHILE MANAGING THE EMOTIONAL TOLL OF ODD** ... 33
   The Emotional Toll on Families: Navigating Stress Together ... 33
   Sibling Dynamics: Promoting Healthy Relationships ... 34
   How to Explain ODD to a Sibling ... 36
   Promoting Positive Interactions Between Siblings ... 38
   Strengthening Parent-Child Relationships ... 43
   Developing Empathy in Children with ODD ... 46
   Importance of Paternal Involvement in Management ... 47
   Building a Support Network: Key Resources for Parents of Children with ODD ... 49

3. BUILDING EFFECTIVE COMMUNICATION
   STRATEGIES   52
   Active Listening to Understand the Root of
   Defiance   52
   Dialogue Openers: Initiating Conversations with
   Your Child   55
   Responding Rather Than Reacting: Techniques to
   Stay Calm   57
   The Role of Non-Verbal Communication in
   Managing ODD   58
   Communication Strategies for Discussing Sensitive
   Topics   60

4. PRACTICAL BEHAVIOR MANAGEMENT
   TECHNIQUES   62
   Establishing Consistent Routines for Better
   Behavior   62
   Positive Reinforcement: Reward Systems
   That Work   64
   Setting Boundaries and Consequences: A Balanced
   Approach   65
   De-Escalation Techniques for High-Tension
   Situations   66
   A Personalized De-Escalation Plan Using Specific
   Phrases   67
   The Impact of School Settings on ODD Behaviors   68

5. THERAPEUTIC APPROACHES AND
   INTERVENTIONS   70
   Cognitive-Behavioral Therapy: A Guide for Parents   70
   Family Therapy: Healing Together   72
   Social Skills Training for Children with ODD:
   Integration into Daily Life   73
   The Benefits of Play Therapy   75
   Integrating Mindfulness and Relaxation Techniques   77

6. NAVIGATING EDUCATION AND LEGAL RIGHTS   82
   Collaborating with Schools: Advocating for Your
   Child's Needs   82
   Understanding IEPs and 504 Plans   85
   Navigating Bullying and Social Challenges at
   School   86

Legal Rights for Children with ODD 87
Preparing for Parent-Teacher Meetings Effectively 89

7. THE ROLE OF DIET AND NUTRITION IN MANAGING ODD 91
Nutrition's Impact on ODD: What Parents Need to Know 91
Scientific Studies Suggest Nutrient Deficiencies Can Exacerbate Symptoms of ODD 95
Using Functional Medicine Practitioners vs. General Healthcare Providers 98
Impact of Common Environmental Allergens on Children with ODD 104
Creating a Diet Plan for Children with ODD 107
Nourishing Recipes for Emotional and Behavioral Support: A Family-Friendly Meal Plan 108
The Importance of Lifestyle Changes in Managing ODD Symptoms 113
Integrating Diet and Lifestyle for Comprehensive ODD Management 117

8. THE ROLE OF PHYSICAL ACTIVITY IN MANAGING ODD 118
The Benefits of Physical Activity 118
Structuring a Home Environment Conducive to Well-Being 121
The Influence of Screen Time and Digital Devices 124
Research Studies on School-Based Physical Activity Programs and ODD 128
Examples of Physical Activities for Children with ODD 129
Integrating Physical Activity Into Daily Routine 130
Beginner-Friendly Physical Activities 131
Creating Fun and Engaging Physical Activities 132
Engaging Activities That Feel Like Play 135
Tips for Encouraging Participation 136

9. SELF-CARE FOR PARENTS 138
Recognizing Signs of Parental Burnout 139
Strategies for Managing Parental Stress 140

Building a Support Network: Finding and Using Resources	142
Building a Support Network for Parents	144
10. ADDRESSING COMMON QUESTIONS AND CONCERNS	146
"What If I've Tried Everything?": Addressing Despair	147
Managing Judgment from Outsiders	148
Discerning the Right Time for Professional Help	150
Adjusting Techniques as Children Grow	151
Overcoming Resistance to Change Within the Family	153
Dealing with the Stigma of Medication	154
Strategies for Single Parents Managing ODD	155
Ensuring Consistency Across Different Caregivers	156
Conclusion: A Holistic Approach of Resilience, Empathy, and Advocacy	161
References	165

INTRODUCTION

The sun barely rises, and you're already feeling the tension of what today might bring. Your child, diagnosed with Oppositional Defiant Disorder (ODD), is likely to start the day with a battle—a refusal to get ready for school, perhaps, or a shouting match over breakfast. The emotional rollercoaster is exhausting. Yet amidst these daily disruptions, there are moments of deep connection and understanding—small victories that give you hope and push you to keep going. This book is dedicated to expanding those moments of hope, guiding you through the complexities of ODD, and equipping you with strategies to nurture a more peaceful home.

The purpose of this book is clear: to offer you, the parent or caregiver, a detailed toolkit filled with evidence-based strategies, real-life examples, and insights into managing the day-to-day challenges posed by ODD. More than that, it's a source of support, emphasizing the important role of self-care and nurturing the parent-child relationship. Each chapter builds on the previous one to form a comprehensive guide to transform your family dynamics.

My journey to write this book stems from a deep passion for helping families like yours. I am not just a professional in this field; I genuinely empathize with your daily struggles. Over the years, I've seen many families transform their lives, moving from chaos to calm, and I am committed to helping you achieve similar results. This book combines practical advice with a compassionate understanding of your realities, aiming to be a beacon of hope and a valuable tool in your parenting journey.

As we progress, you'll find this book is a lifeline for those who feel overwhelmed and unsupported. We will tackle common misconceptions about ODD, clarify coexisting conditions, and discuss everything from behavior management techniques to navigating educational and legal challenges. Importantly, we will focus on you as well—the parent—offering strategies for maintaining your well-being while managing the demands of parenting a child with ODD.

Let me share a story that resonated deeply to give you a taste of the journey ahead. A few years ago, I worked with a family who felt utterly defeated by their son's defiant behavior. By consistently applying the techniques outlined in this book, they improved their son's behavior and strengthened their family bond. Their story is one of many that inspire the chapters of this book, each filled with actionable advice grounded in the latest research and clinical wisdom.

This book acknowledges the diverse dynamics of modern families. Whether you're a single parent, part of a blended family, or navigating the complexities of multiple children, the strategies here are designed for you. They are inclusive, adaptable, and rooted in the principle that every family can achieve a more tranquil home environment.

Though the road may seem daunting, there is a path forward. This book is your map and companion to guide you toward a relationship with your child defined by understanding, respect, and love. Prepare to feel empowered, equipped, and, above all, hopeful. Together, we can turn daily disruptions into opportunities for growth and connection. Welcome to your journey toward a more peaceful home.

CHAPTER 1
UNDERSTANDING ODD, ITS SYMPTOMS, AND HOW IT DIFFERS FROM OTHER BEHAVIORAL DISORDERS

Parenting a child with Oppositional Defiant Disorder can feel overwhelming, like navigating an endless maze where each turn brings new challenges and uncertainties. As a parent, you may often find yourself questioning how to support your child best while managing the daily struggles that ODD presents. This chapter guides you through that maze, offering practical insights to help you understand the full spectrum of ODD symptoms. This chapter aims to empower you by connecting with your challenges and providing clear distinctions between typical childhood behaviors and those driven by ODD. With this knowledge, you'll be better equipped to respond effectively, avoiding common pitfalls such as misdiagnosis or strategies that might inadvertently worsen the situation at home.

DECODING THE SYMPTOMS OF ODD: BEYOND DEFIANCE

ODD often reveals itself through a child's defiant behavior toward authority figures, which is the most visible and widely recognized symptom. However, ODD encompasses much more than just defiance. It includes a broad spectrum of behaviors, such as pronounced irritability, frequent and intense temper tantrums, and a persistent pattern of vindictiveness that lasts for at least six months. Children with ODD may appear unusually angry for their age and can be spiteful or vindictive, often acting deliberately to annoy others or seek revenge. These behaviors are more intense and occur more frequently than in a child's typical developmental stage.

Understanding the difference between ODD and typical behavioral challenges in children is essential. While it's normal for children to display defiant behavior at times, such as during the "terrible twos" or teenage years, the key distinction lies in the frequency and severity of these behaviors—children with ODD exhibit challenging behaviors with greater consistency and intensity than their peers.

For example, while many children might throw tantrums, those with ODD may experience severe outbursts multiple times a day, significantly disrupting their daily functioning. These outbursts represent a persistent pattern that can seriously strain the child's relationships at home and school. Understanding this persistence and intensity is essential for identifying ODD and responding appropriately.

HOW ODD DIFFERS FROM OTHER BEHAVIORAL DISORDERS AND COMMON COEXISTING CONDITIONS

ODD often overlaps with other behavioral disorders, but it has distinct symptoms, underlying causes, and treatment approaches. Below, we compare ODD with different conditions to clarify how it stands apart while also addressing common coexisting conditions like anxiety and mood disorders.

Oppositional Defiant Disorder (ODD)

- **Core Features:** ODD is characterized by an angry, irritable mood, defiant behavior, and vindictiveness, primarily directed at authority figures such as parents or teachers. These behaviors go beyond typical childhood defiance and cause significant problems in daily life.
- **Behavioral Focus:** Defiance is aimed at authority, but children with ODD are not typically aggressive toward others or involved in severe violations of social norms (unlike Conduct Disorder).
- **Emotional Dysregulation:** Children with ODD often have difficulty managing their emotions, leading to frequent temper tantrums and persistent irritability.

Attention-Deficit/Hyperactivity Disorder (ADHD)

- **Core Features:** ADHD involves difficulties with inattention, hyperactivity, and impulsivity. Children may struggle to focus, sit still, or control impulses.

- **Behavioral Focus:** ADHD-related behaviors are driven by attention and activity issues rather than defiance. Children with ADHD may appear oppositional but often because they find it difficult to focus or follow directions.
- **Overlap With ODD:** ADHD and ODD often co-occur. Impulsivity in ADHD can intensify defiant behaviors, but defiance itself is not a core part of ADHD.

Autism Spectrum Disorder (ASD)

- **Core Features:** ASD is marked by difficulties in social communication, repetitive behaviors, and strong preferences for routines. Children may struggle to read social cues, engage in repetitive actions, or focus intensely on specific interests.
- **Behavioral Focus:** Behaviors in ASD are often linked to challenges with communication and change in routine rather than intentional defiance. While children with ASD may appear oppositional when their routine is disrupted, the behavior is often a response to stress rather than defiance.
- **Overlap with ODD:** Some children with ASD may display oppositional behaviors, especially in reaction to frustration or sensory overload. However, these behaviors are often a result of communication struggles rather than the oppositional nature typical of ODD.

Anxiety Disorders

- **Core Features:** Anxiety disorders involve persistent feelings of worry or fear, which can manifest as avoidance, irritability, or even defiance.

- **Behavioral Focus:** A child with ODD and anxiety may act out due to defiance and also as a response to underlying fears. This can make their behavior unpredictable, as they may be reacting to anxiety rather than solely opposing authority.
- **Overlap with ODD:** Anxiety can heighten the child's emotional sensitivity, making defiant behaviors more erratic and more challenging to manage. It's important to recognize that anxiety may be driving some of the defiance, which requires a more nuanced approach to management.

Mood Disorders (Including Depression)

- **Core Features:** Mood disorders, such as depression, involve persistent sadness, irritability, or feelings of hopelessness.
- **Behavioral Focus:** A child with both ODD and depression may show increased irritability and hostility, which can worsen their oppositional behaviors. Emotional struggles like sadness can deepen the anger and defiance commonly seen in ODD.
- **Overlap with ODD:** When combined with ODD, mood disorders make managing defiance more challenging because emotional lows can trigger more severe outbursts or hostility.

Asperger's Syndrome (Now Part of ASD)

- **Core Features:** Asperger's Syndrome, now classified under Autism Spectrum Disorder, involves challenges in social interaction, nonverbal communication, and repetitive

behaviors. Unlike other forms of autism, individuals with Asperger's do not typically experience language or cognitive delays.
- **Behavioral Focus:** Like ASD, behaviors in Asperger's are often tied to difficulties with social interaction and adherence to routine. These behaviors are not inherently defiant or oppositional.
- **Overlap with ODD:** Children with Asperger's may resist changes in routine or display rigid thinking, which can sometimes be misinterpreted as defiance. However, their resistance is rooted in a need for routine rather than a deliberate oppositional mindset.

Conduct Disorder (CD)

- **Core Features:** Conduct Disorder is more severe than ODD and involves behaviors that violate societal norms and the rights of others, such as physical aggression, destruction of property, or serious rule violations.
- **Behavioral Focus:** CD involves aggression, bullying, and antisocial behavior, going beyond the defiance seen in ODD. While ODD defiance is directed at authority figures, CD involves more widespread disruptive behavior.
- **Overlap with ODD:** ODD can sometimes lead to Conduct Disorder if left untreated, though not all children with ODD progress to CD. Conduct Disorder is more extreme, with aggressive and antisocial behaviors defining the condition.

UNDERSTANDING OVERLAP AND INTERPLAY BETWEEN DISORDERS

When ODD coexists with conditions like anxiety, mood disorders, or ADHD, it amplifies the challenges a child faces. For example:

- A child with both ADHD and ODD may have impulse control issues, leading them to interrupt classes. When corrected, they may respond with defiance, escalating the situation.
- A child with Anxiety and ODD might act out to oppose authority and also because they feel anxious or scared, making their defiance more unpredictable.
- A child with Depression and ODD might struggle with deep irritability and sadness, which can make managing oppositional behaviors much more difficult, as emotional lows often fuel more intense defiance.

By understanding how ODD differs from other disorders and how coexisting conditions impact behavior, you can better tailor your approach to helping your child manage their challenges.

UNDERSTANDING THE BIOLOGICAL BASIS OF ODD

Research shows that children with ODD often have differences in specific brain functions, particularly those associated with emotional regulation and impulse control. Neuroimaging studies have observed that some children with ODD may have an imbalance in neurotransmitters—the chemicals that help transmit signals in the brain—which can affect their ability to manage impulses and emotions effectively. This biological underpinning highlights that the behaviors associated with ODD are not simply a matter of choice or willfulness on the child's part but are manifestations of underlying neurodevelopmental issues.

Brain Function and Structure

Prefrontal Cortex and Emotional Regulation

- The prefrontal cortex helps manage behavior, emotions, and impulses.
- In children with ODD, this area may develop slower or work less effectively, making it harder for them to control anger or frustration.
- They may struggle to hold back aggressive or defiant reactions when faced with stressful situations.

Studies show that children with ODD have reduced activity in the prefrontal cortex, leading to impulsive outbursts and defiance.

Amygdala and Emotional Reactions

- The amygdala handles emotions like fear and aggression.
- In children with ODD, the amygdala can be overactive, causing exaggerated emotional reactions to perceived threats or frustrations.
- This may explain why minor frustrations trigger big outbursts in children with ODD.

Neurotransmitter Imbalances and Impulse Control

Dopamine and Reward Processing

- Dopamine regulates mood and motivation, particularly related to rewards.
- Children with ODD may have abnormal dopamine signaling, making it harder for them to control impulses and focus on long-term rewards.
- As a result, they may respond less to positive reinforcement, making traditional reward systems less effective in managing their behavior.

Serotonin and Aggression

- Serotonin helps regulate mood and aggression.
- Low serotonin levels have been linked to increased impulsivity and aggression in children with ODD.
- This may cause them to react with defiance and irritability, especially in stressful situations or when faced with minor frustrations.

In summary, the biological basis of ODD shows that these children aren't simply being defiant by choice. Fundamental differences in brain function and neurotransmitter levels influence their behavior.

RECOGNIZING AND UNDERSTANDING THE EARLY SIGNS AND PROGRESSION OF OPPOSITIONAL DEFIANT DISORDER

Identifying the early signs of ODD is key to seeking timely intervention and managing the disorder effectively. ODD typically appears before a child turns eight and sometimes as early as preschool. Early indicators may include:

- Persistent stubbornness
- Frequent refusal to follow directions
- Unwillingness to compromise or negotiate with others

If left unaddressed, these behaviors can develop into more severe defiance and hostility as the child ages.

Progression of ODD

As ODD progresses, defiant behaviors often intensify. Early signs may include:

- **Frequent temper tantrums:** Intense anger or frustration leading to prolonged outbursts that are disproportionate to the situation.
- **Argumentativeness:** Constantly challenging rules, instructions, or decisions.
- **Refusal to comply:** Persistent rejection of reasonable requests, even when clearly communicated.

Provocative and Irritable Behavior

Children with ODD may also display behaviors intended to provoke or annoy others, such as:

- **Blaming others:** Shifting responsibility for mistakes or misbehavior onto someone else.
- **Vindictive actions**: Holding grudges or seeking revenge for perceived wrongs.
- **Irritability:** Overreacting to minor frustrations with prolonged anger and resentment.

Emotional and Social Challenges

Children with ODD often have difficulty managing emotions, which can affect their relationships and lead to social isolation. Other common challenges include:

- **Impulsivity:** Acting without considering consequences can lead to conflicts at home or school.
- **Mood swings:** Rapid shifts between anger, frustration, and defiance.
- **Difficulty accepting blame:** Regularly avoiding responsibility for conflicts or misbehavior.
- **Lack of empathy:** Showing little concern for how their actions impact others, with minimal remorse for hurtful behavior.

Uncooperative Behavior

Children with ODD frequently resist cooperation and may deliberately do the opposite of what is asked. Additional signs include:

- **Excessive complaining:** Regular dissatisfaction with rules or tasks, often expressed in a negative or oppositional tone.
- **Difficulty with transitions:** Struggling to move from one activity to another, often reacting with frustration or anger.

These behaviors can result in frequent peer conflicts, leading to further social issues.

Next Steps

If these symptoms persist for six months or more across various settings (home, school, or social environments), seeking an evaluation from a mental health professional may be beneficial. Early diagnosis and intervention can lead to better management of ODD and improve outcomes for both the child and the family.

Documenting these behaviors can provide valuable insights. Keeping detailed records of when and how these behaviors occur will help understand their development and formulate effective management strategies. This, in turn, can create a more supportive and structured environment for the child.

CASE STUDY: NAVIGATING LIFE WITH A CHILD DIAGNOSED WITH ODD

Background: Meet Jamie, a seven-year-old boy recently diagnosed with ODD. Jamie's parents have noticed a consistent pattern of defiant and oppositional behavior over the past year, which has significantly impacted his interactions both at home and school. Understanding Jamie's behavior through various everyday scenarios helps show how ODD can manifest differently depending on the setting.

Scenario 1: Playdate at Home

Jamie is excited about having a friend over for a playdate, but his excitement quickly turns into frustration when the friend suggests a game Jamie doesn't like. Jamie insists on playing his favorite game and refuses to compromise. When his friend starts the suggested game without him, Jamie becomes visibly angry, pushes the game pieces off the table, and shouts, "You're not my friend anymore!" Despite attempts from his parents to mediate, Jamie's frustration escalates to the point where the playdate has to be cut short. His friend leaves feeling upset and confused.

ODD Influence: Jamie's inability to compromise and quick escalation into anger are typical of ODD. His rigid thinking and need for control led to a situation where he felt threatened when things didn't go his way, causing him to react with hostility and aggression.

Scenario 2: At School During Group Work

During a group activity in his second-grade class, Jamie is assigned a task he doesn't want to do. He immediately protests, crossing his arms and refusing to participate. The teacher tries to encourage Jamie to contribute, but he responds by arguing, "Why do I have to do it? It's a stupid idea!" Jamie then withdraws from the group, sitting quietly but seething with frustration. Jamie becomes increasingly upset as the group continues without him, throwing his pencil across the room and shouting, "This is all dumb!"

ODD Influence: In this scenario, Jamie's resistance to participating in the group activity is driven by his oppositional nature. His Defiance escalates as he feels increasingly cornered by the teacher's requests, which leads to an outburst that disrupts the classroom environment.

Scenario 3: Family Outing to a Restaurant

Jamie's family decides to go out for dinner at a restaurant. From the beginning, Jamie is resistant, complaining about the choice of restaurant. When his parents ask him to put away his tablet during the meal, Jamie responds with a loud "No!" and begins to argue. As his parents try to enforce the request, Jamie's behavior becomes more disruptive; he starts kicking the chair, making loud noises, and refusing to eat. The situation becomes so difficult that the family leaves the restaurant early, feeling embarrassed and stressed.

ODD Influence: Jamie's Defiance in this scenario is triggered by a perceived restriction of his freedom (being asked to put away his tablet). His aggressive response to a simple request exemplifies the oppositional behaviors typical of ODD, particularly in situations where he feels a lack of control or autonomy.

Summary: Through these scenarios, Jamie's behavior demonstrates the key characteristics of ODD: persistent Defiance, difficulty managing frustration, and a tendency to escalate conflicts. Each situation illustrates how ODD can affect a child's life, from social interactions to school performance and family activities. Understanding these patterns is vital for developing strategies to help Jamie and others like him navigate their challenges more effectively, ultimately leading to better outcomes for the child and their family.

OBSERVATION AND DOCUMENTATION PROCESS

Effectively managing ODD begins with careful observation and systematic documentation of your child's behaviors. This process provides a clear understanding of the patterns and triggers associated with ODD, allowing for more informed and effective interventions. Here's a step-by-step guide to help you navigate this process:

1. Establish a Baseline

Duration: Begin by consistently observing your child over a set period, such as two weeks, to gather a comprehensive picture of their behavior.

Setting: Note the different environments where behaviors occur—home, school, or social settings. The context in which behaviors arise can offer important insights.

2. Create a Behavior Log

Format: Record your observations in a structured behavior log. This log can be a notebook, spreadsheet, or even a dedicated behavior-tracking app.

Key Categories to Document:

- Date and Time: Record when the behavior occurred.
- Location: Identify where the behavior took place (e.g., home, school)
- Antecedent: Note what happened immediately before the behavior, identifying potential triggers.
- Behavior: Provide a detailed description of the behavior.
- Consequence: Document what happened immediately after the behavior.
- Duration: Track how long the behavior lasted.
- Intensity: Rate the intensity of the behavior on a scale (e.g., 1-5).

3. Example Entries for Behavior Log

Example 1:

- Date and Time: July 20, 2024, 3:00 PM
- Location: Home (living room)
- Antecedent: The child was asked to turn off the TV and start homework.
- Behavior: The child yelled, "I don't want to!" and threw a pencil across the room.
- Consequence: The parent calmly reiterated the request and set a timer for a five-minute break before starting homework.
- Duration: 10 minutes (from initial request to starting homework).
- Intensity: 3 (moderate Defiance, mild aggression).

Example 2:

- Date and Time: July 21, 2024, 9:30 AM
- Location: School (classroom)
- Antecedent: The teacher asked the class to line up for recess.
- Behavior: The child refused to line up, crossed arms, and sat on the floor.
- Consequence: The teacher gave the child a choice between lining up and missing the first five minutes of recess. The child eventually complied.
- Duration: 5 minutes (from compliance request).
- Intensity: 2 (mild defiance, no aggression).

Example 3:

- Date and Time: July 22, 2024, 12:20 PM
- Location: Home (kitchen)
- Antecedent: Lunch was served with a vegetable the child dislikes.
- Behavior: The child shouted, "I hate this!" and pushed the plate away.
- Consequence: The parent acknowledged the dislike, asked the child to try one bite, and offered an alternative vegetable if the first was refused.
- Duration: 15 minutes (from the start of lunch to settling down).
- Intensity: 4 (high Defiance, moderate aggression).

4. Weekly Summary

Patterns: Regularly review the behavior logs to identify any emerging patterns, such as common triggers or specific times of day when defiant behavior is more likely.

Frequency: Monitor how often specific behaviors occur to understand their consistency.

Progress: Track changes over time to assess whether certain behaviors increase or decrease in frequency, duration, or intensity.

5. Analysis and Strategy Formulation

Identify Triggers: Use the documented antecedents to pinpoint common triggers that may lead to defiant behavior.

Develop Strategies: Based on the patterns observed, create strategies to manage or prevent these behaviors. For instance, if homework time frequently triggers Defiance, consider implementing a structured routine with regular breaks to ease the transition.

Collaborate with Professionals: Share your behavior logs with therapists, educators, or other professionals to gain additional insights and tailor your approach based on expert recommendations.

6. Review and Adjust

Regular Review: Periodically revisit your behavior logs to evaluate the effectiveness of your implemented strategies.

Adjustments: Be prepared to tweak your strategies based on your child's progress and any new patterns that emerge, ensuring that your approach remains dynamic and responsive to your child's needs.

You can gather invaluable insights into their ODD by systematically observing and documenting your child's behaviors. This process helps identify effective management strategies and track progress over time.

The Importance of Accurate Observation

Misunderstanding or misinterpreting ODD symptoms can lead to severe consequences, such as misdiagnosis or ineffective treatment plans. Harsh disciplinary measures may exacerbate defiant behaviors rather than improve them. In contrast, approaches emphasizing communication, problem-solving, and understanding can yield much better outcomes. By fully understanding the spectrum of ODD symptoms, you can implement more tailored and effective interventions, reduce stress on family dynamics, and enhance the overall atmosphere at home.

THE MISCONCEPTIONS OF ODD: DEBUNKING HARMFUL MYTHS

One of the most significant barriers to understanding and effectively treating ODD is the widespread presence of myths and misconceptions. These misunderstandings distort public perception and create stigma, leaving families feeling isolated and hesitant to seek help. To better understand and support those affected, it's essential to debunk these harmful myths with accurate information.

Myth 1: ODD Is Just Bad Parenting

The Myth: Children with ODD act out because their parents are too lenient or inconsistent with discipline.

The Fact: While parenting styles can influence behavior, ODD is a complex disorder with multiple contributing factors, including genetics, neurobiology, and environmental influences. Effective parenting strategies can help manage symptoms, but blaming parents oversimplifies the issue and ignores the disorder's true complexity.

Myth 2: ODD Is Just a Phase

The Myth: Children with ODD are simply going through a rebellious phase that they will outgrow.

The Fact: ODD is a persistent and disruptive pattern of behavior that goes beyond typical childhood defiance. It requires recognition and appropriate intervention. Without treatment, children with ODD are at risk of developing more severe behavioral and mental health issues.

Myth 3: Children with ODD Are Just Looking for Attention

The Myth: The behaviors associated with ODD are merely attention-seeking actions that can be ignored or disciplined away.

The Fact: Children with ODD exhibit defiance, anger, and vindictiveness as part of a psychological disorder, not simply to gain attention. Ignoring these behaviors can lead to escalation, and punitive measures are often ineffective. Professional guidance and structured behavior management plans are necessary.

Myth 4: ODD Is Rare

The Myth: ODD is uncommon and not something most people will encounter.

The Fact: ODD is one of the most common behavioral disorders in children, affecting approximately 3 to 5% of the population. Increased awareness and understanding can lead to better identification and support for affected children and their families.

Myth 5: ODD Is the Same as ADHD

The Myth: ODD and ADHD are essentially the same disorders because both involve disruptive behaviors.

The Fact: While ODD and ADHD can co-occur and share some symptoms, they are distinct disorders. ADHD is mainly characterized by inattention, hyperactivity, and impulsivity, while ODD is marked by a consistent pattern of angry, defiant, and vindictive behavior. Treatment approaches for each disorder differ and should be tailored to the child's specific needs.

Myth 6: Children with ODD Are Deliberately Disobedient

The Myth: Kids with ODD choose to be defiant and can control their behavior if they want to.

The Fact: The behaviors associated with ODD are symptoms of a disorder, not simply choices. Children with ODD often struggle with emotional regulation and impulse control, making it difficult for them to comply with demands and manage their reactions. Understanding this can lead to more effective support strategies.

Myth 7: ODD Can Be Fixed with Medication Alone

The Myth: Medication is a quick fix for managing ODD behaviors.

The Fact: While medication can be helpful, especially if there are co-occurring conditions like ADHD, it is not a standalone solution for ODD. Behavioral therapies, parent training, and comprehensive treatment plans are essential for effectively managing ODD.

The Importance of Debunking Myths

Dispelling these misconceptions is fundamental for providing accurate information, reducing stigma, and promoting effective interventions. Understanding ODD as a complex disorder requiring a multifaceted approach can help parents, educators, and professionals better support children in overcoming the challenges associated with this condition. By replacing myths with facts, we can create a more compassionate and informed environment that fosters understanding and encourages effective, tailored interventions for children with ODD.

CHAPTER 2
STRENGTHENING FAMILY RELATIONSHIPS WHILE MANAGING THE EMOTIONAL TOLL OF ODD

This chapter explores the emotional and psychological strain ODD places on parents, siblings, and marital relationships. By understanding these dynamics and implementing effective strategies, families can navigate the challenges together, building resilience and leading to a supportive, unified environment.

THE EMOTIONAL TOLL ON FAMILIES: NAVIGATING STRESS TOGETHER

Parenting a child with Oppositional Defiant Disorder can bring intense emotional strain, often leaving parents feeling drained and helpless. The stress may manifest physically as insomnia, fatigue, and headaches. Emotionally, parents often struggle with anxiety, depression, or self-doubt, questioning their ability to handle the situation.

Marital relationships may suffer, as disagreements over managing the child's behavior can lead to conflict. Maintaining a united front is critical. Open communication and regular discussions about parenting strategies help reduce tension. Couples or family therapy can also provide support, allowing parents to work together to address the challenges ODD presents.

Feelings of guilt and isolation are also common. Parents may blame themselves for their child's difficulties or feel distanced from friends and family who don't fully understand their situation. Recognizing these feelings is key, and connecting with a support network or other parents facing similar challenges can help alleviate the burden.

Building family resilience is essential to navigating ODD. Strategies like family game nights, outdoor activities, and counseling can help strengthen family bonds. Educating all family members about ODD ensures a collective approach and creates a healthier home environment, encouraging patience, understanding, and support.

SIBLING DYNAMICS: PROMOTING HEALTHY RELATIONSHIPS

Siblings of a child with ODD often experience emotional challenges of their own, such as feelings of neglect, jealousy, or frustration. Siblings may feel overlooked because parental attention is required to manage the ODD child's behavior. Some might even act out to gain more attention and mimic the negative behaviors they observe.

Educating siblings about ODD is fundamental for developing empathy and support within the family. Using age-appropriate explanations, parents can help siblings understand that the child with ODD isn't deliberately misbehaving but is struggling with a disorder. Younger children may benefit from simple analogies, such as comparing the brain to a computer that occasionally malfunctions, causing unpredictable behaviors. Older siblings can better grasp how emotions and reactions are affected by ODD.

Another critical strategy is encouraging teamwork between siblings. Cooperative activities, such as building puzzles, playing team sports, or working on creative projects together, can stimulate a sense of camaraderie and mutual respect. Highlighting and praising moments of cooperation reinforces positive behavior and helps siblings build solid and supportive relationships.

Case Study 1: Using a Reward System to Encourage Positive Sibling Interactions

The Thompson family faced sibling rivalry after their son, Liam, was diagnosed with ODD. His younger sister, Emma, began imitating his defiant behavior to get more attention. To address this, the parents implemented a reward system encouraging positive interactions. Liam and Emma earned stars for cooperative activities, such as playing games or helping each other with tasks. When they earned enough stars, the family enjoyed a shared reward, like a trip to the zoo. Over time, the reward system reduced sibling rivalry and increased cooperation.

Key Takeaway: Reward systems can encourage positive sibling interactions by reinforcing teamwork and shared experiences and shifting focus from competition to cooperation.

Case Study 2: Family Meetings to Address and Prevent Sibling Resentment

The Rodriguez family noticed that their older daughter, Sofia, felt resentful toward her brother, Mateo, who has ODD. To address this, the parents began holding weekly family meetings where everyone could express their feelings. This allowed Sofia to share how Mateo's behavior impacted her, and the parents took the time to explain ODD in terms she could understand. The meetings also provided a space for developing strategies to improve family interactions. As a result, Sofia's resentment diminished, and the family grew closer.

Key Takeaway: Regular family meetings allow siblings to express their feelings, encourage empathy, and reduce resentment by ensuring all voices are heard.

HOW TO EXPLAIN ODD TO A SIBLING

As expressed above, helping a sibling understand ODD is an important step to promote empathy and support within the family. Use simple terms and relatable analogies to explain that the challenging behaviors associated with ODD are symptoms of a disorder, not intentional actions. Here are some practical ways to communicate this:

Analogies to Explain ODD

- **The Broken Leg Analogy:** Just as a person with a broken leg can't walk properly, a person with ODD struggles to control their behavior and emotions.

- **The Overloaded Circuit Analogy:** Sometimes, their brain becomes overwhelmed, leading to emotional and behavioral challenges.
- **The Stormy Weather Analogy:** Although their emotions can be unpredictable, they will eventually pass, like a storm.
- **The Allergy Analogy:** Just as someone with a peanut allergy reacts differently to peanuts, someone with ODD responds differently to certain situations.
- **The Brain Traffic Analogy:** Their brain is like a busy street with too much "traffic," making it hard to think clearly.
- **The Volcano Analogy:** Their emotions build up like pressure in a volcano, eventually leading to an "eruption."

Practical Tips for Siblings

- **Be Patient:** Encourage patience and remind them that their sibling's difficult moments will pass.
- **Show Support:** Inspire kindness and understanding, knowing their sibling is struggling.
- **Communicate:** Tell siblings they can talk to parents or a trusted adult if they feel upset or confused.

Reassuring the Sibling

- **Focus on Positive Traits:** Help the sibling recognize the positive aspects of their relationship and their sibling's strengths.
- **Empathy and Understanding:** Assist empathy by helping them understand that their sibling is not being difficult on purpose.

These analogies and tips can help siblings develop a more compassionate and supportive attitude toward their brother or sister with ODD, leading to a more harmonious and understanding family environment.

PROMOTING POSITIVE INTERACTIONS BETWEEN SIBLINGS

Encouraging positive interactions among siblings can help maintain harmony within the family. This is because engaging in activities that cater to all your children's interests and abilities ensures that no one feels left out. Neutral, enjoyable settings—such as family game nights, outdoor sports, or creative art projects—allow siblings to connect without the focus being solely on ODD. Here are some guidelines for promoting these interactions.

1. **Set Clear Expectations and Rules**
   - **Consistency**: Establish consistent rules and expectations for all siblings to follow. Make sure everyone understands and agrees with these guidelines.
   - **Fairness**: Apply the rules equally to all siblings to prevent feelings of favoritism or resentment.
2. **Encourage Cooperative Activities**
   - **Shared Interests**: To promote shared experiences, identify activities that all siblings enjoy, such as board games, sports, or creative projects.
   - **Teamwork Tasks**: To boost cooperation and positive interaction, assign tasks requiring teamwork, such as building a puzzle or cooking a simple meal.

3. **Model Positive Behavior**
   - **Role Modeling**: Demonstrate positive communication, conflict resolution, and empathy in your interactions with your children.
   - **Praise and Recognition**: Acknowledge and praise positive interactions and cooperation when you see them, reinforcing good behavior.
4. **Teach and Reinforce Social Skills**
   - **Conflict Resolution**: Teach siblings how to resolve conflicts peacefully, using techniques like "I" statements and active listening.
   - **Emotional Regulation**: Help them develop strategies for managing their emotions, such as deep breathing or taking a break when feeling overwhelmed.

"I" statements are a communication technique to express feelings or concerns without blaming or criticizing the other person. They focus on the speaker's feelings, making the conversation less confrontational and likely to lead to resolution. By using "I" statements, individuals can express their emotions and needs clearly while reducing the other person's defensiveness.

The typical structure of an "I" statement is:

"I feel [emotion] when [specific behavior] because [reason or impact]."

For example:

- Instead of saying, "You never listen to me," you could say, "I feel frustrated when I talk and you look at your phone because it seems like you're not paying attention."

- Instead of, "You're always bossy," you might say, "I feel upset when I'm not included in decisions because I want to feel like my opinions matter."

This approach helps nurture more productive and respectful conversations, especially when resolving conflicts among siblings or family members.

5. **Promote Empathy and Understanding**
   - **Education**: Explain ODD in simple terms to the sibling without ODD to help them understand that certain behaviors are symptoms of the disorder, not intentional actions.
   - **Perspective Taking**: To promote empathy, encourage siblings to consider how their brother or sister might feel and why they act out.
6. **Create a Special Time for Each Child**
   - **One-on-One Time**: Spend individual time with each child to ensure they feel valued and heard, which can reduce feelings of jealousy or competition.
   - **Family Meetings**: Hold timely family meetings to discuss issues and celebrate successes, reinforcing family unity.
7. **Set Up a Reward System**
   - **Positive Reinforcement**: Establish a reward system where siblings earn incentives for positive interactions and teamwork. This encourages them to focus on cooperation and mutual respect. Rewards can be tailored to each child's interests to make the system more motivating and effective.

- **Joint Rewards**: Create rewards that both siblings can enjoy together, such as a trip to the park, a movie night, or a special outing. These shared experiences reinforce positive behavior, promote bonding, and strengthen their relationship.

8. **Provide Safe Spaces**
    - **Personal Space**: Ensure each child has a designated area to retreat when they need alone time. This personal space is vital for recharging and managing emotions, especially during times of stress.
    - **Calm-Down Areas**: Designate specific areas in your home where family members can go to calm down if they're feeling upset or overwhelmed. These areas should be equipped with comforting items like books, music, or soft furnishings to assist emotional regulation.

9. **Involve Siblings in Problem-Solving**
    - **Collaborative Solutions**: Involve both siblings in finding solutions to conflicts or problems. This process empowers them, promotes mutual respect, and teaches valuable problem-solving skills they can use throughout life.
    - **Family Problem-Solving**: Address recurring issues as a family by brainstorming ways to handle them together. This approach strengthens family bonds and ensures everyone's voice is heard and valued, stimulating a sense of unity and cooperation.

Examples of Activities to Promote Positive Interactions

- **Cooperative Games**: Engage in games that require teamwork and communication, such as building a Lego structure, playing a cooperative board game, or working on a puzzle together. These activities help siblings practice working together toward a common goal.
- **Art Projects**: Work on collaborative projects, such as drawing a mural or creating a scrapbook of family memories. These creative endeavors allow siblings to express themselves while building something meaningful together.
- **Outdoor Activities**: Participate in physical activities like playing catch, riding a bike, or exploring nature together. Outdoor activities are fun and provide a healthy outlet for energy and stress while encouraging positive interactions in a relaxed setting.
- **Storytelling**: Take turns telling parts of a story to create a fun and engaging narrative. This activity promotes imagination, cooperation, listening, and building on each other's ideas.
- **Chore Challenges**: Turn household chores into fun challenges or competitions where siblings work together to achieve a common goal. For example, you can create a "clean-up race" or a "kitchen challenge" where they collaborate to finish tasks efficiently. This makes chores more enjoyable and boosts teamwork.

These shared experiences are powerful tools for building bonds and reducing rivalry, as they create positive memories and promote teamwork. Be sure to monitor interactions during these activities and step in when necessary to guide them to ensure that the moments remain inclusive and supportive for all children involved.

Monitoring Behavioral Influence

Be vigilant for signs that the child with ODD might inadvertently influence their siblings' behavior negatively. This could manifest as mimicking disruptive behaviors or adopting inappropriate coping mechanisms they observe. Early intervention is critical to preventing these issues from escalating.

- **Addressing Negative Influences**: When you notice negative behaviors being mimicked, address them through open discussions. Explain why certain behaviors are unacceptable and reinforce the importance of positive behavior. Setting clear family guidelines on acceptable conduct helps establish boundaries and expectations.
- **Reinforcing Positive Behavior**: Whenever siblings handle difficult situations well, praise and reward their positive behavior. This reinforcement encourages them to continue responding constructively and helps manage immediate challenges and prevent long-term behavioral issues from developing.

STRENGTHENING PARENT-CHILD RELATIONSHIPS

Amidst the demands of daily life, finding time to connect with your child may feel like a challenge. However, these moments of connection are essential for nurturing a strong and supportive relationship. This chapter explores how dedicating quality time to your child can serve as a foundation for a healthier, more harmonious bond, strengthen your relationship, and enhance family dynamics.

Quality Time: Activities to Strengthen Bonds

Plan Regular One-on-One Time: Amid daily life's rush, it's important to carve out consistent, distraction-free time each week for one-on-one activities with each child. This time is not just about physical presence but emotional engagement. Whether it's a walk, quiet reading session, or chat over ice cream, these moments allow your child to feel valued and heard. Letting your child choose the activity empowers them and deepens your connection by revealing their interests and passions.

Activities That Encourage Connection

Tailor activities to your child's interests and developmental stage to enhance the quality of your time together. Younger children might enjoy imaginative play or crafts, while older kids prefer cooking, DIY projects, or exploring nature. Reading together is also a powerful way to connect by opening doors to discussions and shared experiences. The goal is simple outings and meaningful interactions that strengthen your bond.

The Role of Rituals and Traditions

Family rituals and traditions offer security and continuity, especially for children with ODD. These rituals—like weekly game nights, annual trips, or bedtime routines—create predictable patterns in a chaotic world and help children feel grounded and connected. Involve your child in creating these traditions, whether choosing the game for family night or planning a trip. These practices become touchstones of connection and stability.

Assessing and Adapting Activities

Regularly reassess and adapt your shared activities as your child grows to keep them engaged. What appealed at six may not at twelve. Stay flexible, open to trying new things, and willing to pivot if something isn't working. This ongoing dialogue ensures that your time together remains meaningful and shows your child that their preferences matter.

Reflection Section: Quality Time Checklist

- Schedule consistent one-on-one activities each week.
- Let your child choose activities that align with their interests.
- Ensure this time is free from distractions.
- Choose age-appropriate activities that promote connection.
- Establish and maintain family rituals and traditions.
- Regularly adapt activities to stay relevant and engaging.

Prioritizing regular, meaningful interactions lays the foundation for a strong and supportive relationship with your child. This connection helps manage ODD's challenges and boosts a sense of security and belonging vital for your child's overall development.

DEVELOPING EMPATHY IN CHILDREN WITH ODD

Modeling Empathetic Behavior: Children learn empathy by observing the adults around them. Show empathy in your daily interactions—with your child and others. For example, when a friend is going through a tough time, express concern and offer support. Your child will see and begin to understand what it means to care about others' feelings, and this sets the foundation for empathetic behavior in their interactions.

Teaching Emotional Recognition: Helping your child recognize and name their emotions is key to developing empathy. Label emotions during daily interactions, like saying, "I see you're feeling frustrated because your toy broke." This validates their feelings and helps them connect words to emotions. Storybooks or movies can also help, as discussing characters' emotions builds emotional vocabulary and understanding.

Role-Playing Scenarios: Role-playing is a fun, effective way to teach empathy. Set up scenarios where your child practices responding empathetically, such as pretending a friend falls down and gets hurt. Guide your child to react with concern and reinforce empathy in a controlled setting. Reversing roles—where you model a caring response—can further strengthen these skills.

Empathy as a Solution to Conflicts: Empathy can transform how conflicts are handled within the family. Guide your child to consider others' feelings during disagreements, encouraging them to express how they feel and listen to the other person. Model this behavior in your conflicts and show your child how to find solutions that respect everyone's emotions. Over time, this approach helps your child develop a more empathetic and effective way of resolving conflicts.

Imagine a family where empathy is a daily practice. Parents actively demonstrate empathy, and children mimic this in their interactions. They learn to recognize and express emotions, practice responding with kindness, and use empathy to resolve conflicts. This environment creates a more harmonious and supportive family dynamic.

Integrating these strategies into your daily life helps your child develop empathy—a skill that will benefit them in countless ways. This foundation strengthens your relationship with your child and equips them to navigate social interactions more effectively.

IMPORTANCE OF PATERNAL INVOLVEMENT IN MANAGEMENT

Fathers often face unique challenges in engaging with their child's management plan. Societal norms sometimes cast fathers more as disciplinarians than nurturers, creating internal conflicts about how best to support their children. Work commitments and the pressure to provide financially can also limit the time and energy available for day-to-day parenting tasks. However, active paternal involvement offers significant benefits, including better behavioral outcomes for the child and strengthened family dynamics.

Strategies for Engagement: Fathers can increase their involvement by taking on specific routines or tasks related to their child's care, such as establishing a consistent bedtime routine, overseeing homework, or handling morning preparations. Participation in therapy sessions or parent-training programs is another major aspect because it equips fathers with specific strategies for managing ODD behaviors and shows the child that both parents are equally invested in their well-being. Leading weekend activities or special projects can also promote bonding and reinforce the father-child relationship.

Addressing Stigma: Traditional gender roles and societal expectations can create barriers, making it difficult for some fathers to feel comfortable in nurturing roles. Support groups and resources designed specifically for fathers can be invaluable by offering a platform to share experiences, seek advice, and find camaraderie with others facing similar challenges. Encouraging fathers to participate in these resources can help break down stigmas and promote a more inclusive approach to parenting.

Balancing Parenting Roles: Consistent and mutual support between parents is important for managing ODD effectively. Open communication is the foundation of this balance. Parents can divide responsibilities effectively by regularly discussing each other's strengths, challenges, and preferences in parenting tasks. Ensuring that both parents are aligned on strategies and expectations is vital, which might involve setting aside time for regular check-ins to review progress and adjust the management plan as needed. This collaborative approach benefits the child's development and strengthens the partnership between parents.

For example, consider David, who initially struggled to connect with his son, Alex, who was diagnosed with ODD. David learned strategies for managing Alex's behaviors through a father-focused support group. He took charge of the morning routine and transformed it into a positive interaction time. David also attended therapy sessions, which helped him gain insights into Alex's triggers and effective de-escalation techniques. Over time, David's involvement led to noticeable improvements in Alex's behavior and strengthened their bond.

Similarly, John and his wife, Sarah, found that balancing their parenting roles created a more harmonious home environment. John facilitated weekend activities while Sarah maintained consistent daily routines. This division of responsibilities ensured their son, Michael, received balanced support, reinforcing the strategies learned in therapy and strengthening their partnership.

BUILDING A SUPPORT NETWORK: KEY RESOURCES FOR PARENTS OF CHILDREN WITH ODD

There are several well-established online forums, support groups, and therapy programs that can offer guidance and community support for parents of children diagnosed with ODD. These resources provide educational materials, emotional support, and practical advice:

1. **Children and Adults with Attention-Deficit/Hyperactivity Disorder (CHADD)**
    - **Website:** https://chadd.org
    - **Description:** Though CHADD primarily focuses on ADHD, it often overlaps with ODD, as many children have both conditions. CHADD offers local chapters, online communities, and educational materials, including webinars and toolkits for managing disruptive behavior.
    - **Support:** CHADD offers a parent-to-parent support program and forums where parents can connect and share experiences.

2. **The American Academy of Child and Adolescent Psychiatry (AACAP)**
   - **Website:** https://www.aacap.org
   - **Description:** AACAP provides a detailed guide on understanding ODD, treatment options, and how to find professional help. They offer a "Find a Child Psychiatrist" tool to help parents locate specialized professionals.
   - **Support:** Includes resources for finding therapy and treatment and expert advice through online articles and fact sheets.
3. **Parent to Parent USA**
   - **Website:** https://www.p2pusa.org
   - **Description:** Parent to Parent USA is a national network providing emotional and informational support to families of children with special needs, including behavioral disorders like ODD. They connect parents with trained support parents who have experienced similar situations.
   - **Support:** The network offers one-on-one emotional support and resource sharing through local chapters.
4. **National Alliance on Mental Illness (NAMI)**
   - **Website:** https://www.nami.org
   - **Description:** NAMI offers a wealth of information on various mental health disorders, including ODD. Their support groups, both online and in-person, focus on peer support and shared experiences.
   - **Support:** NAMI's Family-to-Family program provides education and support for parents of children with mental health challenges, including behavioral issues like ODD.

5. **Therapist Aid - Behavioral Therapy Worksheets**
    - **Website:** https://www.therapistaid.com
    - **Description:** Therapist Aid provides free, evidence-based worksheets, tools, and resources for parents and therapists working with children diagnosed with behavioral disorders like ODD.
    - **Support:** It includes worksheets for behavior modification, emotional regulation, and communication strategies.

CHAPTER 3
BUILDING EFFECTIVE COMMUNICATION STRATEGIES

I magine this: after a long day, you're finally unwinding, but your child suddenly erupts over a minor issue, leaving you frustrated and helpless. How can you shift this moment from conflict to connection? This chapter dives into practical strategies for building effective communication, starting with the essential skill of active listening.

ACTIVE LISTENING TO UNDERSTAND THE ROOT OF DEFIANCE

Beyond simply hearing words, active listening involves fully engaging with your child's verbal and non-verbal cues. In the whirlwind of daily life, it's easy to respond on autopilot, giving half-hearted nods while your mind races with a thousand other thoughts. However, when dealing with a child who has ODD, this superficial level of engagement won't cut it. Active listening requires you to be present and give your child your undivided attention. It's about capturing the emotions behind their words and acknowledging their feelings, which can help uncover the root causes of their defiance.

To practice active listening effectively, start by maintaining eye contact. This simple act shows your child that you are entirely focused on them, promoting a sense of connection and importance. Nod to show understanding and use verbal affirmations like "I see" or "That sounds frustrating." Avoid interrupting, even if you feel compelled to correct or advise them immediately. Allowing your child to complete their thoughts without interjection validates their feelings and provides a clearer picture of what's driving their behavior.

Validating your child's feelings is essential in making them feel heard and understood. This does not mean you have to agree with their behavior but rather acknowledge their emotions. For instance, if your child is angry about a new rule, you might say, "I can see that you're upset about this new rule. It must feel very frustrating." This approach helps your child feel their emotions are recognized, reducing the intensity of their defiance. By not rushing to offer solutions or judgments, you give them the space to express themselves more openly, which can lead to a deeper understanding of their needs and concerns.

Consider the case of Sarah, a mother who struggled with her son, Jake, whose defiant outbursts were a daily occurrence. Sarah decided to try active listening. One evening, after a particularly heated argument over homework, she sat down with Jake and said, "I want to understand why homework makes you so upset. Can you tell me more about it?" Jake began to speak, initially with anger, but his tone softened as Sarah listened without interruption. He revealed that he felt overwhelmed by the amount of work and feared he wouldn't be able to complete it perfectly. This breakthrough allowed Sarah to address Jake's anxiety about failure rather than just the surface-level defiance.

Active listening can transform your interactions with your child by turning conflicts into opportunities for connection and problem-solving.

Reflective Listening Exercise

- **Choose a Calm Moment:** Pick a time when you and your child are relatively calm.
- **Initiate the Conversation:** Start with an open-ended question, "Can you tell me what's been bothering you lately?"
- **Maintain Eye Contact:** Look into your child's eyes, showing them your full attention.
- **Listen Without Interruption:** Let your child speak freely without cutting in. Nod and give verbal cues like "I understand" to show you're engaged.
- **Validate Their Feelings:** Reflect on what you've heard. For example, "It sounds like you're upset because you feel it's unfair."
- **Avoid Immediate Solutions:** Resist the urge to solve the problem immediately. Instead, listen and acknowledge their feelings.

Integrating active listening into your daily interactions builds trust and understanding. This helps de-escalate defiant behaviors and creates a stronger, more empathetic relationship with your child. The journey to effective communication is a series of small, consistent efforts that pave the way for significant improvements in your family dynamics.

DIALOGUE OPENERS: INITIATING CONVERSATIONS WITH YOUR CHILD

Initiating discussions in the middle of high-stress or distracting environments can lead to more conflict than resolution. Instead, choose a calm, quiet moment when you are relatively relaxed. This could be during a walk in the park, while sharing a meal, or even during bedtime routines. The goal is to create an environment where your child feels safe and less defensive, making them more likely to open up.

Open-ended questions are your best friends in these conversations. They invite your child to share more than just a yes or no answer, opening the door to deeper discussions. Instead of asking, "Did you have a good day at school?" try, "Can you tell me about the best part of your day?" or "What was something that frustrated you today?" These questions encourage your child to elaborate on their experiences and emotions, giving you valuable insights into their world. By showing genuine interest in their responses, you promote trust and understanding.

Sharing your feelings and experiences can also encourage your child to open up. Children often model their behavior on their parents, so when you share your stories, you demonstrate that talking about emotions and challenges is okay. For example, if you're discussing how hard it is to stay calm during stressful situations, you might say, "You know, I also get frustrated sometimes when things don't go as planned. It helps me to talk about it. How about you?" This approach normalizes the act of sharing and helps your child see that you understand what they're going through.

Role-playing exercises can be another effective tool in preparing for these conversations. Learning to initiate and navigate difficult discussions can make you feel more confident and prepared. You might role-play with a partner or in front of a mirror, focusing on maintaining a calm tone, using open-ended questions, and validating feelings. This practice helps you internalize the techniques, making implementing them easier in real-life situations.

Consider a scenario where Laura, a mother of two, constantly argued with her teenage daughter, Emma, over screen time limits. Instead of the usual confrontations, Laura decided to change her approach. She sat down with Emma on a quiet Saturday morning, away from the typical evening chaos. Laura opened the conversation by saying, "I've noticed we've been arguing about screen time. Can you tell me how you feel about the new rules?" Surprised by the calm approach, Emma shared her frustrations and concerns. Laura listened, shared her challenges with balancing screen time, and brainstormed solutions. This approach resolved the immediate conflict and improved their overall communication.

Creating a habit of using these dialogue openers can transform how you and your child interact. It turns confrontations into conversations and strengthens a relationship built on mutual respect and understanding. As you practice these techniques, they will gradually become more intuitive, making it easier to address issues before they escalate into serious conflicts. The aim is to make your child feel heard and understood and reduce their need to resort to defiance as a means of communication.

RESPONDING RATHER THAN REACTING: TECHNIQUES TO STAY CALM

Handling tense situations with control begins with recognizing your triggers—actions or words that provoke strong emotional reactions. For instance, disrespectful language or raised voices might cause you to react impulsively. Reflecting on these moments and identifying patterns (perhaps by journaling) can help you develop strategies like taking a timeout to respond thoughtfully rather than reacting on instinct.

Targeted breathing is one effective tool for staying calm in stressful situations. The 4-7-8 technique—inhaling for four counts, holding for seven, and exhaling for eight—helps soothe the nervous system and gives you a brief moment of reflection before responding. This pause can significantly improve how you handle interactions with your child.

Another essential technique is the "STOP" framework: Stop, Take a breath, Observe your feelings, and Proceed with kindness. This promotes mindfulness and enables you to respond more thoughtfully rather than being overwhelmed by the heat of the moment.

Previously, in Chapter 2, we introduced "I" statements—a method to express emotions without escalating conflict. Instead of pointing fingers or blaming your child, these statements focus on your feelings and how behavior affects you, encouraging open communication. If you haven't yet integrated this approach into your conversations, it's an excellent way to maintain calm during challenging moments. For example, rather than saying, "You always interrupt me," try, "I feel upset when I'm interrupted because I need focus to complete my work." This approach reduces defensiveness and creates space for constructive dialogue.

For example, imagine you're preparing dinner and your child starts yelling about a lost toy. Instead of snapping back, you recognize your stress trigger, take a deep breath, and calmly suggest working together to find the toy. This models problem-solving and emotional regulation for your child while helping you stay calm.

Consider Mark, a father who faced frequent interruptions from his daughter while working from home. He identified his trigger—work deadlines—and implemented the pause technique to manage his frustration. When his daughter interrupted, he used an "I" statement: "I feel stressed when I'm interrupted during work. Can we set a time to talk about what you need?" This simple shift helped reduce his stress and opened the door to better communication with his daughter.

THE ROLE OF NON-VERBAL COMMUNICATION IN MANAGING ODD

Imagine this scenario: You ask your child to put away their toys, but your crossed arms and tense voice send a mixed message that might escalate the situation. Nonverbal cues—such as body language, facial expressions, and tone of voice—play a critical role in how your child interprets your words. When these cues are positive, they can help de-escalate tension. But if they contradict your words, they can lead to confusion and defiance.

To promote better behavior, try modeling positive non-verbal communication. Imagine using an open posture, maintaining a calm tone, and offering a gentle smile when asking your child to do something. These non-verbal signals demonstrate respect and calmness, encouraging your child to mirror these behaviors in their interactions. For example, if you stay calm during a disagreement, your child is more likely to learn how to manage their emotions similarly.

It's also important to interpret your child's non-verbal signals. Children with ODD may not always verbalize their feelings, but their body language can speak volumes. Signs like avoiding eye contact, clenching fists, or a furrowed brow can indicate frustration or anger. You can better understand their emotional state and respond more effectively by paying attention to these cues. For instance, if your child avoids eye contact and withdraws, it might signal they feel overwhelmed or anxious. Acknowledging these cues can help you address their needs before things escalate by giving them space to calm down or using soothing words to reassure them.

Consistency between your verbal and non-verbal messages is necessary. Telling your child everything is fine while your facial expression says otherwise can create mistrust and anxiety. Ensuring your words align with your non-verbal cues builds reliability and trust. For example, if you tell your child you understand their frustration, ensure your tone and facial expressions reflect empathy and understanding. This alignment reinforces your message and makes it easier for your child to comprehend and accept.

Consider Paul, a father who struggled with his son Tommy's frequent outbursts. Paul realized that his tense body language and raised voice fueled Tommy's defiance. By consciously adopting a more relaxed posture and speaking calmly and steadily, Paul noticed a significant improvement in their interactions. Tommy began to mirror his father's calm demeanor, leading to fewer outbursts and more constructive conversations. This change in nonverbal communication improved their relationship and created a more peaceful home environment.

Mastering non-verbal communication can transform your interactions with your child. Modeling positive behaviors, interpreting your child's cues, and ensuring consistency between what you say and how you say it lays the groundwork for trust and understanding. This approach helps manage defiant behaviors and strengthens your relationship with your child.

COMMUNICATION STRATEGIES FOR DISCUSSING SENSITIVE TOPICS

When discussing sensitive topics with your child, preparation and timing are important. It matters not just what you say but how and when you say it. Begin by organizing your thoughts and anticipating your child's possible reactions. Consider how they might feel —defensive, upset, or confused—and prepare yourself emotionally to handle these responses with empathy.

Establishing a safe, non-judgmental environment is key for productive conversations. Opt for a setting where your child feels at ease, such as a cozy corner at home or during a relaxed walk. The aim is to make your child feel secure enough to express themselves without fear of judgment or punishment. Start with a supportive statement, such as, "I want to understand how you're feeling about what happened yesterday."

Using empathetic language is critical to making your child feel understood. Instead of issuing commands, express understanding of their feelings. For example, rather than saying, "You need to stop acting out," try, "I see that you're frustrated, and I want to help you figure out why." This approach shifts the focus from simply addressing behavior to understanding the underlying emotions, which promotes a more supportive atmosphere.

Follow-up is just as necessary as the initial conversation. After discussing a sensitive issue, check in with your child later to see how they process the conversation. Simple questions like, "How are you feeling about our talk?" or "Is there anything else you'd like to discuss?" show your commitment to their well-being and reinforce the idea that their feelings matter.

In summary, effective communication about sensitive topics involves:

- Thoughtful preparation
- Creating a safe and non-judgmental space
- Using empathetic language
- Following up to ensure ongoing support

These strategies address the immediate issue, build a foundation of trust and understanding, and transform potential conflicts into opportunities for deeper connections and growth.

CHAPTER 4
PRACTICAL BEHAVIOR MANAGEMENT TECHNIQUES

Imagine it's a Monday morning. You have ten minutes to get everyone out the door, and your child refuses to put on their shoes. The clock is ticking, your stress rises, and a simple task becomes a full-blown battle. Establishing consistent routines can transform these chaotic moments into more manageable ones by providing a sense of security and predictability that reduces defiant behaviors. In this chapter, we'll explore how to create and maintain routines that work for your family and offer a pathway to smoother, more harmonious daily interactions.

ESTABLISHING CONSISTENT ROUTINES FOR BETTER BEHAVIOR

Children with ODD often thrive on structure. Consistent routines provide a framework that helps reduce the unpredictability that triggers anxiety and defiant behavior. A well-structured routine creates a predictable environment where your child knows what to expect and what is expected of them. This decreases anxiety and, over time, can reduce defiant behaviors.

Case Study: Morning Routine Transformation

Consider the case of Angela, who struggled every morning with getting her son Max to cooperate. Max resisted simple tasks like getting dressed or eating breakfast, often leading to meltdowns. Angela implemented a more structured morning routine, with each task clearly outlined and scheduled. She involved Max in the process by letting him choose the order of tasks. Within a couple of weeks, the meltdowns decreased as Max felt more in control of his morning. The routine reduced his anxiety about what would happen next, which led to smoother mornings for both.

Start by mapping out a daily routine that includes essential activities like wake-up times, meals, homework, play, and bedtime. For example, mornings could consist of waking up at 7 AM, having breakfast at 7:30 AM, and leaving for school at 8 AM. After school could be a snack at 3:30 PM, homework at 4 PM, and playtime until dinner at 6 PM. The key is consistency—stick to these times as much as possible to create a reliable rhythm.

However, balancing consistency with flexibility is critical. Sometimes, life gets in the way of routines, and rigidity can lead to more stress. If unexpected events arise, calmly communicate changes to the schedule to teach your child adaptability. This flexibility helps them manage their expectations and reduces anxiety when things don't go as planned.

Actionable Step: Involve your child in creating the schedule. Giving them input into their routine helps them feel more in control and reduces defiant behaviors. Ask for their input, such as when they prefer doing homework or what they want to include in their bedtime routine. This collaborative approach supports cooperation and teaches planning skills.

POSITIVE REINFORCEMENT: REWARD SYSTEMS THAT WORK

Positive reinforcement focuses on rewarding desired behaviors rather than punishing defiance. This method is particularly effective for children with ODD because it helps them connect good behavior with positive outcomes. Instead of focusing on what your child does wrong, emphasize what they do right.

Case Study: The Power of Praise

Lisa, a mother of two, struggled with her son Jordan's refusal to complete his chores. Instead of nagging, she started a reward chart where Jordan earned points for each chore completed without argument. Over time, Jordan became more motivated to help out around the house. At first, he was excited to earn small rewards like extra playtime, but soon, Lisa noticed he enjoyed the praise and recognition even more. This shift in focus from punishment to reward dramatically reduced the power struggles over chores.

While tangible rewards like toys or treats are effective, verbal praise or extra playtime can also be powerful motivators. For example, a points system where your child earns points for completing chores or homework can be used. These points can then be traded for a family outing or another privilege—the key is to ensure that the rewards are meaningful to your child.

Consistency is vital when using positive reinforcement. Reward the behavior immediately and consistently to strengthen the connection between actions and outcomes. Avoid over-reliance on tangible rewards, as verbal praise and recognition of effort boost intrinsic motivation over time.

Actionable Step: Create a points system or reward chart to track positive behaviors. Praise effort as much as the outcome to encourage perseverance and self-worth.

SETTING BOUNDARIES AND CONSEQUENCES: A BALANCED APPROACH

Clear boundaries and predictable consequences help children with ODD feel secure. For example, instead of saying, "Behave yourself," be specific: "Please finish your homework before playing video games." When boundaries are specific, children understand what's expected of them and are more likely to comply.

Case Study: Setting Boundaries with Flexibility

John and Sarah were struggling with their son Ethan's screen time habits. They noticed that taking away his tablet when he hadn't completed homework often led to explosive outbursts. So, they sat down with Ethan to set clear rules—homework must be completed before screen time, but he could take a break during homework if needed. Giving Ethan some control over how he followed the rules made a big difference. When he chose to take a break, he didn't lose the privilege of screen time later, and this reduced his oppositional reactions to the rules.

The consequences of breaking boundaries should be appropriate and directly related to the behavior. For instance, if your child fails to follow the rules about homework before TV, they lose TV privileges in the evening. Consistency in applying these consequences is critical—sporadic enforcement can confuse your child and make the rules feel arbitrary.

Involving your child in setting boundaries can also reduce defiant behaviors. When children feel they have a say in the rules that govern their lives, they are more likely to respect them.

Actionable Step: Regularly review boundaries and consequences with your child, especially as they grow. Encourage their input on rules, such as screen time limits, and adjust them as your child demonstrates more responsibility.

DE-ESCALATION TECHNIQUES FOR HIGH-TENSION SITUATIONS

Despite your best efforts with routines and positive reinforcement, there will still be moments of escalation. Recognizing early warning signs, such as clenched fists, raised voices, or pacing, can help you intervene before defiance escalates into a meltdown.

Case Study: Using a Calm Approach

In one situation, Mark noticed his son, Ryan, becoming increasingly agitated when asked to finish his homework. Mark noticed Ryan pacing and raising his voice. Instead of reacting defensively, Mark remained calm, using slow, deliberate speech and open body language. He used the 4-7-8 breathing method to center himself before speaking to Ryan. Mark asked, "Would you like to take a break before continuing?" This simple acknowledgment of Ryan's growing frustration helped defuse the situation. Ryan took the break and later returned to complete his homework without further resistance.

Maintaining a calm and controlled response is key. Breathing techniques like the 4-7-8 method—inhaling for four counts, hold for seven, exhale for eight—can calm your nervous system and model emotional regulation for your child. Open body language (e.g., uncrossed arms, relaxed shoulders) and a steady, calm tone also help defuse tension.

The techniques discussed earlier in this chapter on consistent routines can naturally reduce the need for de-escalation. When your child feels more secure and knows what to expect in their day-to-day life, moments of escalation are less frequent. Additionally, "positive reinforcement" discussed earlier can preempt defiance by rewarding good behavior early.

Actionable Steps:

- Develop a personalized de-escalation plan with your child.
- Identify their triggers and decide on calming strategies together, such as deep breathing, listening to music, or retreating to a quiet space.
- Regularly review and practice this plan when emotions are calm.

A PERSONALIZED DE-ESCALATION PLAN USING SPECIFIC PHRASES

When a child with ODD is escalating, using clear and empathetic language can help. Some examples of effective phrases include:

- Acknowledge Feelings: "I can see you're upset right now."
- Empathize: "I understand this is hard for you."
- Provide Choices: "Would you like to talk about it now or in five minutes?"
- Encourage Calmness: "Let's take a few deep breaths together."

Case Study: Effective Language in Action

Maya often felt frustrated when her daughter Lily's behavior escalated into defiance. One day, when Lily was upset over not being allowed to go out with friends, Maya calmly said, "I can see you're angry about this decision. Let's sit and talk when you're ready." Instead of arguing, Lily eventually calmed down and returned to talk about her feelings. By acknowledging Lily's emotions and offering a choice, Maya avoided escalating the conflict.

The key is to remain calm, consistent, and empathetic.

Actionable Step: Practice using these phrases during calm moments so they become second nature in high-tension situations.

THE IMPACT OF SCHOOL SETTINGS ON ODD BEHAVIORS

The school environment can significantly impact a child's behavior. Overstimulating settings or negative peer interactions can exacerbate defiant behaviors. A structured, supportive classroom can help mitigate these challenges.

Case Study: Collaboration with Teachers

Nina's son, Alex, was struggling in school due to his ODD. His teachers reported disruptive behavior, especially during transitions between activities. After discussing Alex's challenges with his teachers, Nina advocated for a seating arrangement near the front, where Alex could avoid distractions. They also created a visual schedule for Alex to follow, which helped him anticipate transitions better. These small changes dramatically reduced Alex's disruptive behaviors, and the collaboration between Nina and the school created a more supportive environment for Alex's learning.

Advocating for changes like tailored seating arrangements, IEPs, or 504 plans can help your child feel more in control and supported. Regular communication with teachers ensures that the strategies you use at home are reinforced in the classroom.

Actionable Step: Schedule regular check-ins with your child's teachers to stay updated on their progress and collaborate on any needed modifications.

Integrating consistent routines, positive reinforcement, clear boundaries, and personalized de-escalation techniques creates a comprehensive framework for managing ODD behaviors. These tools promote your child's sense of security, predictability, and emotional regulation.

CHAPTER 5
THERAPEUTIC APPROACHES AND INTERVENTIONS

This chapter introduces Cognitive-Behavioral Therapy (CBT). This well-researched therapeutic approach offers practical strategies to help children with ODD modify their thoughts and behaviors, leading to better emotional regulation and social functioning.

COGNITIVE-BEHAVIORAL THERAPY: A GUIDE FOR PARENTS

Cognitive-Behavioral Therapy (CBT) is a structured, goal-oriented approach that helps children with ODD understand the connection between their thoughts, feelings, and behaviors. Core techniques, such as problem-solving skills training and cognitive restructuring, empower children to challenge negative thoughts and develop healthier behavioral responses. By reinforcing these techniques at home, parents can ensure that the strategies learned in therapy become consistent parts of daily life, which is vital for maintaining progress. By integrating these techniques into everyday routines, parents can help their child apply therapeutic insights in real-world situations, reinforcing positive behavioral changes. To further support this process, maintaining a behavior journal can offer valuable insights into progress and help guide adjustments as needed.

Behavior Journal

1. **Identify Target Behaviors:** Choose specific behaviors you want to track, such as outbursts, defiance, or cooperation.
2. **Set Clear Goals:** Define progress for each target behavior (e.g., reducing outbursts from daily to weekly).
3. **Daily Tracking:** Record instances of target behaviors, noting the context and any triggers.
4. **Weekly Review:** Summarize the week's data and look for patterns or improvements.
5. **Adjust Strategies:** Discuss any necessary adjustments with your child's therapist based on the review.

Case Study: Alex's Journey to Emotional Control

Alex, a 10-year-old boy with ODD, struggled with frequent outbursts during school and at home. His parents and therapist introduced a behavior journal as part of his CBT program, where Alex tracked his emotional triggers and behaviors. Over time, Alex learned that his outbursts often stemmed from feeling overwhelmed by homework. With the help of his therapist, Alex began using problem-solving skills to manage his homework load and break it down into smaller tasks. His outbursts gradually decreased, and he started to feel more in control of his emotions, which resulted in improved behavior at school and home.

While CBT focuses on the child's internal processes and individual behavior, family therapy expands on these strategies by addressing the broader family dynamics that influence behavior.

FAMILY THERAPY: HEALING TOGETHER

Family therapy complements CBT by improving communication and relationships within the family unit. This approach ensures that the progress made in CBT is supported and reinforced by the entire family, creating a cohesive and nurturing environment. Techniques like active listening and problem-solving in family therapy help families work together to manage ODD more effectively and reduce household tension.

Consider the story of the Cisneros family, who felt trapped in a cycle of conflict due to their son Emilio's ODD. Family therapy taught them to communicate more effectively, set clear boundaries, and support each other better. The parents discovered that their unresolved issues were contributing to the tension, and by addressing these, they created a more harmonious environment for their children. Emilio's siblings, who initially felt neglected, found their voices in the therapy sessions and learned how to support their brother rather than resent him. This collective healing process improved Emilio's behavior and strengthened the family.

As family therapy strengthens the home environment, social skills training further supports the child's ability to navigate interactions outside the family, particularly in school and peer settings.

SOCIAL SKILLS TRAINING FOR CHILDREN WITH ODD: INTEGRATION INTO DAILY LIFE

Social skills training, building on CBT and family therapy, teaches children with ODD how to interact positively with others. Understanding social cues, taking turns in conversation, and managing conflicts can improve relationships and reduce defiant behaviors. This training is reinforced at home and school, where frequent social interactions occur.

Scenarios and Integration at Home

Scenario 1: Understanding Social Cues

You might notice that your child often needs to be more accurate in their facial expressions or body language at home, as it leads to misunderstandings. To help develop this skill, practice by watching a TV show together, pausing to discuss what each character might feel based on their expressions or actions. For example, if a character crosses their arms and frowns, ask your child, "What do you think this character is feeling right now?" This helps them learn to associate particular body language with specific emotions.

Scenario 2: Turn-Taking in Conversation

During family meals, practice turn-taking by encouraging your child to wait until others have finished speaking before sharing their thoughts. If they interrupt, gently remind them of the importance of listening to others and waiting for their turn. You can also set up a game where each family member has to wait for their turn to speak, using a "talking stick" so only the person holding it can talk. This reinforces patience and respect in conversations.

Scenario 3: Managing Conflicts

Suppose your child becomes upset when a sibling takes a toy without asking. Instead of reacting with anger, engage in role-play on how to handle the situation. Guide your child to say, "I feel upset when you take my toy without asking. Can we share it or take turns?" By practicing these responses, they learn to manage conflicts more constructively.

Scenarios and Integration at School

Scenario 1: Recognizing Social Cues

In a classroom setting, teachers can integrate social skills training by having your child participate in group activities that involve recognizing peers' emotions. For instance, during a group project, the teacher might ask your child to observe their classmates' feelings and report back. This encourages them to pay attention to social cues in real time.

Scenario 2: Turn-Taking in Play

Your child can practice turn-taking at recess by playing games like "Simon Says" or taking turns on playground equipment. Teachers and aides can praise your child for waiting their turn and encourage positive peer interactions, reinforcing these behaviors.

Scenario 3: Conflict Resolution in School

If your child encounters a conflict with a classmate, the teacher can intervene by guiding both children through a structured resolution process. This might involve each child stating their perspective, discussing their feelings, and jointly developing a solution. This reinforces the conflict management strategies they have been learning at home.

Case Study: Lily's Growth in Social Skills and Patience

Lily, an eight-year-old girl with ODD, frequently interrupted her peers and struggled with turn-taking. Through social skills training at school and home, she participated in role-playing exercises to learn how to wait her turn during conversations. Lily practiced using a "talking stick" at family dinners to take turns speaking. Over time, Lily improved her interactions with family and friends, resulting in fewer conflicts and more positive peer relationships.

By integrating social skills training into daily interactions at home and school, children can gradually develop the ability to navigate social situations more effectively, leading to improved relationships and fewer conflicts. This holistic approach ensures that skills learned in therapy are consistently reinforced, and this helps children with ODD thrive in various social settings. Just as social skills training enhances external interactions, play therapy allows younger children to explore and express emotions, which can be integrated with other therapeutic approaches.

THE BENEFITS OF PLAY THERAPY

Play therapy mainly benefits younger children, allowing them to express their emotions through creative play. This approach complements CBT and family therapy by providing a safe space for children to process experiences and develop emotional resilience. Play therapy techniques, such as role-playing and storytelling, align with the skills taught in CBT, making it a natural extension of cognitive and behavioral interventions.

Techniques in Play Therapy

Role-Playing: Children act out scenarios that reflect real-life experiences, helping them explore different outcomes and behaviors. For example, using dolls to reenact a school conflict provides insight into their perspective.

Storytelling: Creating stories allows children to mirror their struggles and find ways to cope with difficult situations.

Creative Arts: Drawing, painting, or clay modeling helps children express emotions they might be unable to verbalize. This can offer valuable insights into their emotional state.

Integrating Play Therapy with Other Approaches

Combining play therapy with CBT or family therapy offers a more comprehensive treatment strategy. While play therapy helps children express and process emotions, CBT provides practical skills to manage them. For example, a child might first explore a conflict through play and then work with the therapist to challenge negative thoughts. Family therapy involves parents and siblings and ensures the child feels supported by their family.

Case Study: Ethan's Path to Emotional Expression Through Play

Ethan, a six-year-old with ODD, found it difficult to express his emotions verbally. During play therapy, his therapist introduced storytelling and role-playing exercises to help Ethan process his emotions. He used toy figures to act out conflicts he experienced with classmates, and through these sessions, Ethan learned how to express his feelings constructively. His parents noticed a marked improvement in his communication ability, and his tantrums became less frequent as he gained better emotional awareness through play therapy.

Finding a Qualified Play Therapist

Look for therapists certified by organizations like the Association for Play Therapy (APT), indicating specialized training in play therapy techniques. Seek therapists experienced with children with ODD. When meeting potential therapists, inquire about their approach to play therapy, how they integrate it with other treatments, and how they involve parents. Observe how your child interacts with the therapist to ensure a good fit, indicated by the child's comfort and engagement.

INTEGRATING MINDFULNESS AND RELAXATION TECHNIQUES

Mindfulness and relaxation techniques provide children practical ways to manage stress and improve emotional regulation. Techniques, such as deep breathing and guided imagery, can be easily incorporated into daily routines to complement the strategies learned in CBT, family therapy, and play therapy. Regular mindfulness has been shown to reduce anxiety symptoms and improve attention, as supported by studies like those conducted by Kabat-Zinn et al. (1992) on the impact of mindfulness-based stress reduction programs.

Double Inhale Breathing Exercises Can Reduce Anxiety

Research supports the idea that specific breathing techniques, including double inhales followed by slow exhales, can reduce anxiety. Dr. Andrew Huberman's "physiological sigh," a method discussed in further detail below, effectively reduces physiological stress markers. This technique aligns with findings from research on the autonomic nervous system, which shows that controlled breathing patterns can activate the parasympathetic nervous system and promote relaxation (Huberman, 2021).

Concept of Physiological Sigh

The physiological sigh involves a double inhale through the nose and a slow exhale through the mouth. This method mimics a natural reflex that occurs to optimize lung function and relieve stress. The first inhale fills the lungs with air, while the second, smaller inhale helps to inflate the alveoli, the tiny air sacs in the lungs, which may have collapsed. The prolonged exhale helps expel more carbon dioxide from the body, promoting relaxation and reducing anxiety.

Scientific Basis and Research

Dr. Andrew Huberman, a neuroscientist at Stanford University, has discussed the benefits of the physiological signs on various platforms. His research suggests that this specific breathing pattern can quickly reduce physiological stress markers and promote calmness.

Practical Application of Double Inhale with Slow Exhale

Steps for Physiological Sigh:

1. **Double Inhale**
   1. Take a deep inhale through the nose.
   2. Immediately follow with a second, smaller inhale to expand the lungs fully.

2. **Slow Exhale**
   1. Exhale wholly and slowly through the mouth, ensuring all the air is expelled.

Implementation:

Frequency: Practice this breathing exercise a few times daily, particularly during stress or anxiety.

Duration: Perform the cycle for a few minutes or until a noticeable reduction in anxiety is felt.

Breathing exercises, particularly the physiological sigh (double inhale followed by a slow exhale), have a solid scientific basis for reducing anxiety and promoting relaxation. Research by experts like Dr. Andrew Huberman supports the effectiveness of these techniques in managing stress and enhancing overall emotional well-being. Regular practice can help individuals, including children and adolescents with ODD, manage their anxiety more effectively.

MAKE A DIFFERENCE WITH YOUR REVIEW

UNLOCK THE POWER OF GENEROSITY

"Helping one person might not change the whole world, but it could change the world for one person."

Helping others doesn't always take much—sometimes it's as simple as sharing your thoughts. And it can make a world of difference.

Would you help someone like yourself—someone who's trying to figure out how to handle Oppositional Defiant Disorder (ODD) but feels unsure where to start?

My mission is to make parenting a child with ODD easier, less stressful, and more rewarding for everyone.

But to reach more parents who are searching for answers, I need your help.

Many people choose books based on reviews. By sharing what you think about "The Oppositional Defiant Disorder Guide", you can guide another parent who's in the same shoes you were. Your review could help someone discover new ways to tackle daily disruptions, address defiance, reduce parent burnout, and build stronger family bonds.

So, if this book has helped you, would you mind taking a few minutes to leave a review? You're not just helping me—you're helping other parents, too. Thank you for being part of the journey to a more peaceful home!

Writing a review costs nothing and takes only a few minutes, but it can change the journey for another family just like yours. Your words could help…

…one more parent feel less alone.

…one more family find peace in their home.

…one more child feel understood.

To make a difference, simply scan the QR code below and leave your review:

https://www.amazon.com/review/create-review?asin=B0DMKCCZMM

If helping others matters to you, then you're my kind of person. Thank you from the bottom of my heart!

Michael Karl

CHAPTER 6
NAVIGATING EDUCATION AND LEGAL RIGHTS

Imagine it's the first day of school, and you feel hopeful and anxious. Your child hugs you tightly before hesitantly entering the classroom. As you drive away, you worry about how they'll handle the new environment, expectations, and challenges. To ensure your child is able to thrive, understanding your legal rights and establishing effective communication with the school from the outset is necessary. This chapter provides the tools to help your child thrive in the educational landscape.

COLLABORATING WITH SCHOOLS: ADVOCATING FOR YOUR CHILD'S NEEDS

Building a solid partnership with your child's school is vital for ensuring they receive the support they need. This partnership thrives when parents and educators operate with mutual respect and a shared goal: the child's success. Approach these interactions collaboratively rather than confrontationally, as mutual respect promotes a positive and cooperative atmosphere.

Importance of Mutual Respect

Respectful communication is the cornerstone of a productive relationship with the school. When educators feel respected, they are more likely to be open to your concerns and suggestions. Similarly, when parents feel heard, they're more inclined to trust the school's expertise. This mutual respect helps you navigate challenges and find the best solutions for your child. For instance, when discussing sensitive issues, you might say, "I appreciate all your efforts in supporting my child. I want to discuss additional strategies that could further enhance their success."

Maintaining Open Communication

Open communication keeps everyone informed about your child's progress and any necessary adjustments. Regular updates, such as a communication notebook or weekly email check-ins, can help sustain this ongoing dialogue. This consistent communication keeps everyone aligned, builds trust over time, and ensures that issues are addressed promptly before they escalate.

Creating a Clear Advocacy Plan

Creating a clear advocacy plan is important for adequate support. Document your child's behaviors, triggers, and successful interventions, incorporating insights from professionals. This comprehensive profile gives the school a clear understanding of your child's needs and guides the implementation of necessary accommodations. An advocacy plan acts as a roadmap, ensuring that the school's efforts are focused and effective in supporting your child.

Use Collaborative Language

Frame your requests in a way that champions teamwork. Instead of saying, "You need to do this for my child," try, "How can we work together to support my child in this area?" This approach invites cooperation and shared responsibility.

Acknowledge Educators' Efforts

Start by recognizing the work educators have already done. For example, "I appreciate everything you've done so far, and I think we could build on that by trying…" This acknowledgment shows respect and stimulates a positive dialogue.

Addressing Difficult Topics

When discussing sensitive issues, be direct but empathetic. For example, you might say, "I've noticed my child struggles at certain times of the day. Can we explore what might be causing this and how we can better support them?" This approach balances honesty with compassion and makes it easier to tackle tough topics.

Be Prepared with Solutions

When presenting a concern, come prepared with possible solutions or ask for suggestions. For instance, "I'm concerned about how transitions are handled. What strategies could we try to make these smoother for my child?" This proactive stance demonstrates that you're looking for constructive ways to help.

Collaboration with School Counselors and Special Education Coordinators

Regular meetings with school counselors and special education coordinators are key. They play a pivotal role in your child's education by offering insights into their progress and suggesting additional resources or strategies.

UNDERSTANDING IEPS AND 504 PLANS

IEPs (Individualized Education Programs) and 504 Plans are designed to assist students with disabilities, including those with ODD, by ensuring their educational needs are met. However, they differ in scope, eligibility, and the services they provide.

IEPs are comprehensive plans under IDEA for students whose disabilities significantly impact their educational performance. These plans include detailed evaluations, measurable goals, accommodations, specialized services, and regular reviews. IEPs are designed to provide specialized instruction in the least restrictive environment possible.

Example Scenario for IEP

If a child with ODD struggles significantly with behavior management in the classroom, leading to frequent disruptions in their learning, an IEP might be appropriate. The IEP could include behavioral goals, regular counseling sessions, and specific instructional strategies to address these challenges.

504 Plans focus on providing accommodations to ensure students with disabilities have equal access to education. These plans involve a broader eligibility process, are less formal in their evaluations, and typically do not include special education services. Instead, they ensure necessary modifications and support are needed to help the student succeed in a general education setting.

Example Scenario for 504 Plan

If a child with ODD needs adjustments such as extra time on tests, a quiet space for completing assignments, or preferential seating to minimize distractions, a 504 Plan might be more appropriate. These accommodations help the child access the general curriculum without requiring special education services.

NAVIGATING BULLYING AND SOCIAL CHALLENGES AT SCHOOL

Children with ODD might not express their experiences with bullying, and their defiance can often mask emotional pain. Signs like behavioral changes, increased irritability, or unexplained injuries may indicate bullying. Recognizing these cues is significant in addressing the issue.

When you suspect bullying, have an open, non-judgmental conversation with your child, and document incidents to present to the school. Collaborate with school staff to create a safety plan, such as increased supervision or adjusted schedules.

To improve social integration, practice social skills at home and communicate these strategies to teachers. Encourage participation in structured activities to build friendships. Peer mediation and support groups also offer valuable platforms for resolving conflicts and creating a sense of belonging.

Teaching Self-Advocacy Skills

Empowering children with ODD to advocate for themselves is essential. Teaching them self-advocacy skills helps them express their needs and concerns more effectively. Encourage your child to voice their feelings and preferences constructively. For example, role-playing scenarios where they practice asking for help or expressing discomfort can build their confidence. Self-advocacy supports independence and helps prevent bullying by allowing children to assert themselves in difficult situations.

Addressing bullying, enhancing social skills, teaching self-advocacy, and leveraging peer support can create a safer school environment that assists your child in navigating social interactions confidently.

LEGAL RIGHTS FOR CHILDREN WITH ODD

Navigating the educational system can be challenging, but understanding legal protections like the Individuals with Disabilities Education Act (IDEA) and Section 504 of the Rehabilitation Act can make a significant difference. These laws ensure that children with disabilities receive appropriate educational support, such as IEPs and necessary accommodations.

Real-Life Impact of Legal Advocacy

Consider the case of a child with ODD who was initially denied special education services. The parents, understanding their legal rights under IDEA, advocated for their child, documented behavioral challenges, and sought external evaluations. This led to the school providing an IEP, which included behavioral interventions and modified instruction. As a result, the child's academic performance and school experience improved significantly.

Another example involves a student with ODD who faced disciplinary actions due to their behavior. The parents utilized Section 504 protections to ensure the school implemented behavior modification strategies instead of punitive measures, which led to better outcomes for the student.

Steps to Take if Rights Are Not Respected

If you feel your child's rights are not being respected, start by documenting all interactions with the school, including meetings, emails, and incidents that highlight the issue. This documentation will help you if you need to escalate the situation.

1. **Request a Meeting:** First, request a meeting with school administrators to discuss your concerns and provide documentation.
2. **Seek Mediation:** If the issue remains unresolved, mediation is a non-adversarial approach where a neutral third party helps facilitate a resolution.
3. **Due Process Hearing:** If mediation fails, you can request a hearing, where an impartial officer reviews the case and makes a binding decision.

4. **External Advocacy Support:** Organizations like the Council of Parent Attorneys and Advocates (COPAA) and the National Disability Rights Network (NDRN) offer guidance and representation to uphold your child's educational rights.

Understanding and leveraging these legal protections, documenting issues, and seeking external support when necessary, ensures your child with ODD receives the support needed to succeed in school.

PREPARING FOR PARENT-TEACHER MEETINGS EFFECTIVELY

Effective parent-teacher meetings require clear objectives, constructive communication, and diligent follow-up. To ensure all necessary points are covered, identify key goals, such as discussing behavioral observations or reviewing accommodations.

Managing emotions during these meetings is important, as they can be stressful for parents. Practice deep breathing beforehand, and remind yourself that the goal is collaboration, not confrontation. A trusted friend or advocate can provide emotional support and an additional perspective to help you stay focused and calm.

During the meeting, express concerns constructively and engage in active listening. For instance, instead of stating, "Jamie is always in trouble," say, "Jamie struggles with focus in class. Can we explore strategies to help?" Take notes on key discussions, decisions, and next steps to ensure clarity and accountability.

After the meeting, review your notes, summarize the agreed-upon actions, and share this summary with relevant staff to confirm everyone's understanding. Regularly monitor the progress of the strategies and schedule follow-up meetings as needed. This ongoing communication ensures interventions are effective and responsive to your child's evolving needs.

Setting clear objectives, managing emotions, bringing support, and diligently following up creates a collaborative environment that maximizes the effectiveness of each meeting, ensuring your child receives the support they need.

These strategies provide a solid framework for navigating the educational landscape for your child with ODD. The next chapter will explore the role of diet and lifestyle in managing ODD symptoms, offering practical tips for creating a supportive home environment.

CHAPTER 7
THE ROLE OF DIET AND NUTRITION IN MANAGING ODD

The sun rises, and you find yourself once again preparing breakfast. You watch your child push the cereal bowl away, complaining about the taste. You wonder if what they eat—or refuse to eat—plays a role in their behavior. The link between diet and behavior is compelling, and emerging research highlights how what goes into your child's body can significantly impact their neurological and psychological health. This chapter explores how nutrition and lifestyle choices can be powerful tools in managing ODD symptoms.

NUTRITION'S IMPACT ON ODD: WHAT PARENTS NEED TO KNOW

The gut-brain connection is a compelling area of research that highlights how gut health can significantly influence behavior. The gut and brain communicate through the gut-brain axis, a complex network of neurons, hormones, and microbiota that transmit signals between the digestive system and the brain. An imbalance in gut microbiota can lead to inflammation and affect neurotransmitter production, influencing mood and behavior. For instance, serotonin, a neurotransmitter that regulates mood, is predominantly produced in the gut. Therefore, a healthy gut can contribute to better emotional regulation and reduced behavioral issues in children with ODD.

Identifying potential food triggers is essential for managing ODD symptoms. Since certain foods can exacerbate behavioral issues, pinpointing and eliminating these triggers is essential. Common culprits include sugar, artificial additives, and allergens like gluten and dairy.

Implementing an elimination diet can be an effective way to identify these triggers. Start by removing suspected foods from your child's diet for a few weeks, then gradually reintroduce them one at a time while monitoring for changes in behavior. This process can help you identify which foods may contribute to your child's symptoms, allowing you to make informed dietary choices that support their well-being.

The Role Essential Nutrients Play

Essential nutrients play a significant role in brain health and can improve ODD symptoms. Omega-3 fatty acids—found in salmon and flaxseeds—are essential for brain function and have been shown to reduce symptoms of ADHD, which often coexists with ODD. Zinc—present in foods like beef, pumpkin seeds, and chickpeas—supports neurotransmitter function and can help improve mood and cognitive function. Magnesium—found in leafy greens, nuts, and whole grains—is essential for regulating neurotransmitters and can help reduce anxiety and irritability. Ensuring your child's diet includes these nutrients can support their neurological health and alleviate some ODD symptoms.

The impact of food on mood and behavior is significant—certain foods can directly influence your child's emotional state and behavior. For instance, a diet high in refined sugars can lead to blood sugar spikes and crashes, resulting in mood swings and increased irritability. In contrast, a balanced diet rich in vegetables, fruits, whole grains, and lean proteins can provide a steady supply of nutrients that support stable blood sugar levels and overall brain health. Foods like leafy greens, berries, and whole grains are rich in antioxidants and fiber, which support gut health and reduce inflammation, contributing to better mood regulation and behavior.

Reflection Section: Identifying Food Triggers and Nutritional Needs

- **Keep a Food Diary**: Document what your child eats and note any changes in behavior to help identify patterns and potential food triggers.
- **Plan an Elimination Diet**: Remove common triggers like sugar, gluten, and dairy for two to three weeks. Gradually reintroduce them one at a time, observing any behavioral changes.
- **Incorporate Key Nutrients**: Ensure your child's diet includes Omega-3 fatty acids, zinc, and magnesium. To help with this, consider incorporating foods like salmon, pumpkin seeds, and leafy greens.
- **Monitor and Adjust**: Regularly review your child's diet and adjust based on their responses. Consult with a nutritionist for guidance.

By understanding the gut-brain connection, identifying potential food triggers, and ensuring a diet rich in essential nutrients, you can take significant steps toward managing ODD symptoms through nutrition. This approach supports your child's neurological health and supports a more balanced mood and behavior.

Case Study 1: Mia's Journey with an Elimination Diet

Mia, an eight-year-old girl diagnosed with ODD, exhibited frequent mood swings, defiance, and irritability. Her parents noticed that her behavior often worsened after consuming certain foods, particularly sugary snacks and processed meals. They decided to work with a functional medicine practitioner to explore dietary changes that could help manage Mia's symptoms.

The first step was implementing an elimination diet. Mia's parents removed common potential triggers, including sugar, gluten, and dairy, from her diet for four weeks. Mia's behavior significantly improved during this period, with fewer tantrums and better cooperation at home and school. After reintroducing each food group one at a time, they observed that gluten and high-sugar foods would consistently lead to a return of defiant behaviors within a few hours of consumption.

With the help of their practitioner, Mia's parents designed a gluten-free, low-sugar diet rich in whole grains, lean proteins, and vegetables. They incorporated sweet potatoes, brown rice, chicken, leafy greens, and berries into her daily meals. Her mood stabilized, and her school performance improved dramatically. Emily's parents also introduced omega-3 supplements to her routine, which further supported her emotional regulation.

Mia's family continues to monitor her diet; with these changes, they've seen lasting improvements in her behavior. The dietary adjustments helped reduce her defiant outbursts and improve her attention span and social interactions.

SCIENTIFIC STUDIES SUGGEST NUTRIENT DEFICIENCIES CAN EXACERBATE SYMPTOMS OF ODD

Nutrient deficiencies can impact brain function, emotional regulation, and behavior, potentially worsening the symptoms of ODD. Here are some essential nutrients that have been studied relating to behavioral and emotional disorders, including ODD.

1. Omega-3 Fatty Acids

Omega Omega-3 fatty acids, particularly eicosapentaenoic acid (EPA) and docosahexaenoic acid (DHA), are essential for brain health and function. Research has shown that deficiencies in these fatty acids may lead to increased behavioral problems and emotional dysregulation in children. For instance, a study published in the *Journal of Child Psychology and Psychiatry* found that omega-3 supplementation improved behavioral issues in children with ADHD, which often co-occurs with ODD (Raine et al. 2015, 509-520).

2. Vitamin D

Vitamin D is important for brain development and function, with lower levels linked to increased symptoms of mood disorders and behavioral problems. A study published in *Pediatrics* found that children with lower vitamin D levels were more likely to display aggressive behaviors and symptoms of Conduct Disorder, which shares traits with ODD (Villamor et al., 2019).

3. Iron

Iron deficiency, which can lead to anemia, is associated with cognitive and behavioral issues in children, including increased irritability, poor attention, and behavioral problems. A study published in *Pediatric Research* found that iron supplementation improved cognitive function and behavior in children with low iron levels (AAP Publications, MDPI).

4. Zinc

Zinc is important for brain function and neurotransmitter regulation, and deficiencies in zinc have been linked to behavioral problems and increased hyperactivity. A study published in the *Journal of Child and Adolescent Psychopharmacology* showed that zinc supplementation reduced hyperactivity and impulsivity in children with ADHD, suggesting it may also benefit those with ODD (Bilici et al., 2004).

5. Magnesium

Magnesium is vital for nerve transmission and muscle function, and low magnesium levels can contribute to irritability, anxiety, and restlessness. A study published in *Magnesium Research* found that magnesium supplementation improved behavioral issues in children with ADHD, suggesting it could also benefit children with ODD (Mousain-Bosc et al., 2006).

6. B Vitamins

B vitamins, particularly B6, B9 (folate), and B12, are important for brain health and neurotransmitter function, with deficiencies linked to mood disorders and behavioral issues. A study published in the *American Journal of Clinical Nutrition* found that B vitamin supplementation improved mood and cognitive function in children, indicating potential benefits for managing ODD symptoms (Vyas et al., 2024).

Important Considerations

While direct studies specifically linking nutrient deficiencies to worsening ODD symptoms are limited, there is substantial evidence that deficiencies in essential nutrients like omega-3 fatty acids, vitamin D, iron, zinc, magnesium, and B vitamins can negatively impact children's behavior and emotional regulation. Addressing these deficiencies through diet or supplementation may help improve symptoms in children with ODD by supporting brain function, emotional regulation, and impulse control.

However, remember that supplements are not a standalone solution. They should be considered part of a broader treatment plan, which may include behavioral therapy, parenting strategies, and, in some cases, medication. Every child is different, and the specific needs and potential interactions of supplements can vary. That's why it's essential to consult a healthcare provider before starting new supplements.

Research is ongoing, and while these vitamins and minerals might offer additional support by targeting brain areas and neurotransmitters involved in ODD, more studies are needed to fully understand their impact on ODD-specific symptoms. Always work closely with your healthcare team to develop a treatment plan that addresses your child's unique needs.

Recommendations

Balanced Diet: Ensure that children with ODD receive a balanced diet rich in essential nutrients.

Regular Check-Ups: Regularly monitor nutrient levels through blood tests, mainly if behavioral issues occur.

Functional Medicine Practitioners: Collaborate with functional medicine practitioners to develop tailored dietary plans or consider supplementation if nutrient deficiencies are identified. These experts can help create a holistic approach that addresses nutritional and behavioral aspects to support overall well-being and emotional balance in children with ODD.

USING FUNCTIONAL MEDICINE PRACTITIONERS VS. GENERAL HEALTHCARE PROVIDERS

Functional Medicine Practitioners (FMPs) offer a more holistic and personalized approach to treating children with ODD compared to General Healthcare Providers (GHPs). FMPs focus on the whole child, addressing the root causes of symptoms by considering physical, emotional, and environmental factors, and they develop individualized treatment plans using comprehensive diagnostic tests like blood work. They emphasize nutrition, lifestyle changes, and the integration of multiple therapies into a cohesive plan, while GHPs may focus more on symptom management with standardized protocols. FMPs also prioritize patient education, prevention, and long-term health, spending more time in consultations and collaborating closely with other health professionals, which may need to be more deeply integrated into the GHP approach.

Here's an overview of how FMPs typically operate and their specific roles.

1. Comprehensive Assessment

Detailed History: Functional medicine practitioners begin by thoroughly reviewing the patient's medical history, including family health history, lifestyle, diet, environmental exposures, and psychosocial factors.

Symptom Analysis: They conduct a detailed analysis of the child's symptoms, behaviors, and emerging patterns.

2. Utilizing Blood Work

Nutritional Deficiencies: Blood tests identify deficiencies in essential nutrients such as omega-3 fatty acids, iron, vitamin D, zinc, B vitamins, and magnesium, which play essential roles in brain health and emotional regulation. These nutrients are vital for maintaining cognitive function, supporting neurotransmitter production, and reducing inflammation, all of which are important for managing mood and behavior. In addition to detecting deficiencies, blood tests can also help assess overall nutritional status and guide dietary adjustments or supplementation to address any imbalances and support optimal mental and physical health.

Inflammation Markers: They check for markers of inflammation, such as C-reactive protein (CRP) and homocysteine levels, which can affect brain function and behavior.

Hormonal Imbalances: Blood work can identify hormonal imbalances that might contribute to mood and behavior issues.

Blood Sugar Levels: They assess blood sugar levels and insulin function, as fluctuations in these can impact behavior and mood.

Toxin Exposure: They test for heavy metals and other toxins affecting neurological function.

3. Identifying Underlying Causes

Gut Health: Functional medicine practitioners often examine gut health, including potential dysbiosis or leaky gut syndrome, which can affect mood and behavior through the gut-brain axis.

Food Sensitivities and Allergies: They may test for food sensitivities and allergies that can cause inflammation and impact behavior.

Genetic Factors: Genetic testing can help identify predispositions to certain metabolic or psychological conditions that could influence ODD symptoms.

4. Personalized Treatment Plans

Diet and Nutrition: Based on blood work and other assessments, practitioners develop tailored nutrition plans to address deficiencies and optimize health. These plans may include specific dietary changes, nutritional supplements, and ensuring a balanced intake of macro- and micronutrients.

Supplementation: They recommend supplements to correct deficiencies and support overall brain health and function.

Lifestyle Modifications: Suggestions for improving sleep, physical activity, and stress management to support overall well-being.

Detoxification: If toxins are identified, they provide strategies for reducing exposure and supporting the body's detoxification processes.

5. Ongoing Monitoring and Adjustment

Regular Follow-Ups: Functional medicine practitioners conduct regular follow-ups to monitor progress, adjust treatment plans, and ensure effective interventions.

Dynamic Approach: They adapt the treatment plan as the child's needs change, ensuring a continuous and responsive approach to managing ODD.

Benefits of Functional Medicine in Managing ODD

1. **Holistic Approach:** This approach addresses the whole child, considering physical, emotional, and environmental factors that may influence ODD symptoms.
2. **Root Cause Analysis:** This approach focuses on identifying and addressing the root causes of symptoms rather than just managing the symptoms themselves.
3. **Individualized Care:** This approach provides personalized treatment plans tailored to the specific needs and conditions of the child.
4. **Preventative Focus:** This approach aims to prevent further health issues by promoting overall wellness and addressing underlying dysfunctions early.

Example Scenario

Jake, a 10-year-old diagnosed with ODD, has frequent mood swings and difficulty concentrating. A functional medicine practitioner conducts comprehensive blood work and identifies the following:

- Low levels of omega-3 fatty acids
- Vitamin D deficiency
- High inflammation markers (CRP)
- Potential gluten sensitivity

Based on these findings, the practitioner recommends:

Dietary Changes: Increase omega-3-rich foods like fish, reduce gluten intake, and incorporate more fruits and vegetables.

Supplementation: Use Omega-3, vitamin D, and anti-inflammatory supplements like turmeric.

Lifestyle Modifications: Improving sleep hygiene and incorporating stress-reducing activities like yoga or mindfulness. (We will go into more detail later in the chapter.)

Regular follow-ups show significant improvement in Jake's mood stability and behavior, demonstrating the effectiveness of this holistic and personalized approach.

Case Study 2: Leo's Transformation with Nutritional Supplements and a Balanced Diet

Leo, a nine-year-old boy with ODD, struggled with impulsivity, emotional outbursts, and difficulty concentrating at school. His parents had tried behavioral therapies with some success but wanted to explore how diet could further help manage his symptoms. They consulted a nutritionist specializing in children with behavioral disorders.

After conducting blood tests, the nutritionist found that Leo was deficient in both zinc and magnesium, which are essential for mood regulation and reducing anxiety. Leo's diet was also high in processed foods, including sugary cereals, fast food, and soda, which contributed to erratic energy levels and mood swings.

The nutritionist worked with Leo's family to create a balanced diet plan that included magnesium-rich foods like spinach, almonds, and whole grains and zinc-rich options like pumpkin seeds and chickpeas. They also introduced daily supplements to address the deficiencies. Additionally, Leo's parents removed sugary drinks and processed snacks from the household, replacing them with water, fresh fruits, and nutrient-dense snacks like carrot sticks and hummus.

Within a few weeks of following the new diet and supplement regimen, Leo's parents noticed significant changes in his behavior. His tantrums and emotional outbursts became less frequent, and he was more willing to follow the rules and cooperate at school. His focus during homework sessions improved, and he no longer seemed as easily frustrated by challenging tasks. Over time, Leo's mood stabilized, and his teachers reported better peer interactions and classroom participation.

For Leo, combining dietary changes, particularly eliminating processed foods and correcting nutrient deficiencies, helped manage his ODD symptoms and improve his overall well-being.

In conclusion, functional medicine practitioners use blood work and other diagnostic tools to provide a comprehensive, personalized approach to managing ODD. Identifying and addressing underlying dysfunctions can help improve children's overall well-being and behavior with ODD.

IMPACT OF COMMON ENVIRONMENTAL ALLERGENS ON CHILDREN WITH ODD

Common allergens found in our environments can negatively affect children with Oppositional Defiant Disorder by exacerbating symptoms such as irritability, hyperactivity, and difficulty concentrating. Here are some of the common allergens:

1. Dust Mites

Dust mites are microscopic organisms that thrive in household dust, bedding, upholstery, and carpets. Exposure to dust mites can trigger allergic reactions, leading to respiratory issues, skin irritation, and sleep disturbances. In children with ODD, these symptoms may increase irritability and reduce concentration.

2. Pollen

Pollen from trees, grasses, and weeds is a common outdoor allergen that can easily enter indoor spaces. Pollen allergies may trigger sneezing, runny nose, itchy eyes, and fatigue, potentially worsening mood swings and irritability in children with ODD.

3. Mold

Mold spores, commonly found in damp areas like bathrooms, basements, and kitchens, can cause respiratory problems, headaches, and fatigue. For children with ODD, these health issues may make it harder to manage emotions and behavior.

4. Pet Dander

Pet dander, composed of microscopic skin flakes from animals like cats, dogs, rodents, and birds, easily becomes airborne and settles on surfaces throughout the home. It often includes proteins from saliva,

THE ROLE OF DIET AND NUTRITION IN MANAGING ODD 105

urine, and feces, which can worsen allergic reactions in sensitive individuals. Dander clings to clothing, furniture, and fabrics, making it difficult to remove without thorough cleaning and air filtration. Allergies to pet dander can lead to sneezing, itching, and respiratory issues, increasing stress and irritability in children with ODD.

5. Food Allergens

Common food allergens include peanuts, tree nuts, milk, eggs, wheat, soy, fish, and shellfish. Reactions to these allergens can range from digestive issues and skin rashes to severe anaphylaxis. Food sensitivities and intolerances may also impact mood and behavior, potentially worsening symptoms.

6. Cockroach Droppings

Cockroach droppings and body parts can become airborne allergens, leading to respiratory issues and allergic reactions. In children with ODD, such exposure can contribute to sleep disturbances and increased irritability.

7. Chemical Irritants

Household cleaning products, pesticides, and air fresheners can release volatile organic compounds (VOCs), which may cause headaches, respiratory issues, and skin irritation. These physical discomforts can negatively affect mood and behavior, particularly in children with ODD.

8. Perfumes and Fragrances

Strong scents from perfumes, air fresheners, and scented personal care products can be irritants. Fragrance allergies may trigger headaches, respiratory issues, and skin irritation, increasing stress and irritability.

9. Smoke

Smoke from tobacco, fireplaces, or cooking can be a significant irritant, causing respiratory problems and headaches. For children with ODD, this exposure can increase discomfort and contribute to behavioral issues.

10. Environmental Pollution

Pollutants from industrial sources, vehicle emissions, and urban environments can lead to respiratory issues and fatigue. This type of exposure may worsen symptoms by increasing irritability and reducing focus.

Managing Allergens to Support Children with ODD

To minimize the impact of these allergens on children with ODD, consider the following steps:

Maintain Clean Environments: Regularly clean and vacuum to reduce dust mites, pet dander, and mold.

Use Air Purifiers: Invest in air purifiers with HEPA filters to reduce airborne allergens.

Limit Exposure to Pollen: Keep windows closed during high pollen seasons and use air conditioning.

Choose Hypoallergenic Products: Opt for hypoallergenic bedding, cleaning products, and personal care items.

Manage Food Allergies: Work with a healthcare provider to identify and manage food allergies or sensitivities.

Avoid Smoke and Pollution: Keep the indoor environment smoke-free and reduce exposure to outdoor pollutants.

CREATING A DIET PLAN FOR CHILDREN WITH ODD

Creating a balanced diet for a child can feel overwhelming, but breaking it into manageable steps makes it more accessible. Start by focusing on essential nutrients and eliminating potential triggers. Incorporate a variety of vegetables, fruits, whole grains, and lean proteins while gradually phasing out foods high in sugar, artificial additives, and allergens. This approach supports your child's neurological health without being too drastic.

Engage your child in meal planning and preparation to increase their willingness to try new foods and stick to the plan. Let them choose between healthy options, participate in grocery shopping, and assist with meal prep. This promotes independence and makes mealtime more enjoyable.

Sample meal plans can simplify the process. For breakfast, consider a nutrient-packed smoothie with spinach, berries, and flaxseeds. For lunch, a quinoa salad with greens and grilled chicken might be a good choice, while dinner could feature baked salmon with roasted sweet potatoes and broccoli. Snacks like apple slices with almond butter or carrot sticks with hummus are healthy and appealing.

Monitoring your child's response to the diet is vital. Keep a food diary to track what your child eats and any changes in behavior or mood. This helps identify beneficial foods and those that might trigger adverse reactions. Based on these observations, adjust the diet as needed to ensure it continues to meet your child's evolving needs.

In summary, a balanced diet for a child with ODD requires thoughtful planning, active involvement, and ongoing monitoring. You can effectively support their emotional and behavioral health by focusing on essential nutrients, involving your child in the process, using practical meal plans, and regularly adjusting based on their responses. In the next section, you will find nourishing recipes designed to make healthy eating a shared experience.

NOURISHING RECIPES FOR EMOTIONAL AND BEHAVIORAL SUPPORT: A FAMILY-FRIENDLY MEAL PLAN

While this is not a recipe book, a healthy diet is important, particularly when supporting emotional and behavioral regulation. These simple recipes are designed to provide essential nutrients that may help children with ODD, but they are also great for the entire family. Preparing and enjoying these meals together can benefit your child's health and promote overall family well-being.

1. Grilled Salmon with Quinoa and Spinach Salad (Mediterranean Diet)

Ingredients:

- 2 salmon fillets
- 1 cup quinoa
- 2 cups fresh spinach
- 1/4 cup olive oil
- 1 tablespoon lemon juice
- Salt and pepper to taste

Instructions:

1. Cook quinoa according to package instructions.
2. While quinoa cooks, grill salmon on a pan or grill for 4-5 minutes on each side until fully cooked.
3. Toss spinach with olive oil, lemon juice, salt, and pepper.
4. Serve the grilled salmon on top of quinoa and spinach salad.

2. Flaxseed-Enriched Oatmeal (Omega-3 Rich Diet)

Ingredients:

- 1/2 cup rolled oats
- 1 tablespoon ground flaxseeds
- 1 tablespoon chia seeds
- 1/2 cup almond milk (or other non-dairy milk, such as coconut)
- 1/2 cup water
- 1/4 teaspoon cinnamon
- Optional: Add fresh berries or sliced banana for topping

Instructions:

1. Combine oats, almond milk, water, flaxseeds, and chia seeds in a small saucepan.
2. Cook over medium heat, stirring frequently, until the oatmeal thickens (about 5 minutes).
3. Add cinnamon and top with fresh berries or banana slices.

3. Fresh Fruit Salad with Homemade Yogurt (Elimination Diet)

Ingredients:

- 1 cup strawberries, halved
- 1 cup blueberries
- 1 cup pineapple chunks
- 1 cup plain unsweetened yogurt (you can make homemade or buy)
- 1 tablespoon honey (optional)

Instructions:

1. Combine all fruits in a large bowl.
2. Serve with plain yogurt on the side; drizzle with honey if desired.

4. Lentil and Vegetable Stew (Low-Sugar, Low-Glycemic Diet)

Ingredients:

- 1 cup lentils
- 1 onion, chopped
- 2 carrots, diced
- 1 zucchini, diced
- 2 cups vegetable broth
- 1 can diced tomatoes (no added sugar)
- 1 teaspoon cumin
- Salt and pepper to taste

Instructions:

1. In a large pot, sauté onions, carrots, and zucchini until soft.
2. Add lentils, vegetable broth, and diced tomatoes.
3. Season with cumin, salt, and pepper.
4. Bring to a boil, then simmer for 20-25 minutes until lentils are cooked.
5. Serve with whole-grain bread.

5. Chickpea and Spinach Stir-Fry with Brown Rice (Magnesium and Zinc-Rich Diet)

Ingredients:

- 1 can chickpeas, drained and rinsed
- 2 cups fresh spinach
- 1 cup cooked brown rice
- 1 tablespoon olive oil
- 1 garlic clove, minced
- 1/4 cup pumpkin seeds (for extra zinc)
- Salt and pepper to taste

Instructions:

1. Heat olive oil in a pan, sauté garlic until fragrant.
2. Add chickpeas and cook for 3-4 minutes.
3. Add and stir in spinach and cook until wilted.
4. Serve over brown rice and sprinkle with pumpkin seeds for added zinc.

6. *Kefir Smoothie with Berries and Chia Seeds (Probiotic and Gut-Health-Focused Diet)*

Ingredients:

- 1 cup plain kefir
- 1/2 cup mixed berries (strawberries, blueberries, raspberries)
- 1 tablespoon chia seeds
- 1/2 banana

Instructions:

1. Blend kefir, berries, banana, and chia seeds in a blender until smooth.
2. Serve chilled.

7. *Grilled Chicken with Roasted Sweet Potatoes and Steamed Broccoli (Whole Foods and Balanced Meals)*

Ingredients:

- 2 chicken breasts
- 2 sweet potatoes, diced
- 2 cups broccoli florets
- 1 tablespoon olive oil
- Salt and pepper to taste

Instructions:

1. Preheat oven to 400°F (200°C). Mix sweet potatoes in olive oil, salt, and pepper, then roast for 25 minutes.
2. Grill chicken breasts until cooked through, about 6-7 minutes on each side.
3. Steam broccoli for 5-6 minutes until tender.
4. Serve the chicken alongside the roasted sweet potatoes and steamed broccoli.

These simple and nutritious recipes focus on whole foods, healthy fats, omega-3s, and essential vitamins and minerals. Incorporating these into a daily meal plan can support overall brain health and emotional regulation, helping manage the symptoms associated with ODD. However, it's possible that your child may not like some of the recipes at first, and that's okay. You can gradually introduce individual ingredients into their meals over time, helping them get used to new flavors and textures. These meals are easy to prepare and can be enjoyed by the entire family, making healthy eating a shared experience that benefits everyone.

THE IMPORTANCE OF LIFESTYLE CHANGES IN MANAGING ODD SYMPTOMS

Beyond nutrition, lifestyle factors such as sleep hygiene, physical activity, and structured family routines play an essential role in managing symptoms of ODD. These lifestyle elements are powerful complements to a balanced diet, creating an environment that supports emotional regulation, reduces stress, and promotes positive behavior.

Sleep Hygiene: The Foundation of Emotional Regulation

Children with ODD often struggle with sleep issues, which can exacerbate defiant behaviors, irritability, and emotional dysregulation. Prioritizing good sleep hygiene is essential to managing ODD symptoms.

Why Sleep Matters

Adequate sleep allows the brain to process emotions, repair itself, and regulate behavior more effectively. Children who are sleep-deprived are more likely to experience mood swings, heightened aggression, and lower frustration tolerance.

Example Scenario

Ethan, a seven-year-old boy with ODD, had frequent meltdowns in the mornings, particularly before school. His parents noticed that he often went to bed late and struggled to fall asleep. A therapist recommended a consistent sleep schedule and a calming bedtime routine. They began dimming the lights an hour before bed, limiting screen time, and introducing relaxation techniques like reading a story together. Over a few weeks, Ethan's sleep improved, and his morning outbursts became less frequent as he felt more rested each day.

Sleep Hygiene Tips for Parents

1. **Set a Consistent Sleep Schedule:** Establish a regular bedtime and wake-up time, even on weekends, to regulate your child's internal clock.
2. **Create a Calming Pre-Bedtime Routine:** Reduce screen time, avoid stimulating activities, and encourage quiet activities like reading or listening to calming music.

3. **Ensure a Comfortable Sleep Environment:** Keep the bedroom cool, quiet, and dark. If background sounds are distracting, consider using white noise machines.
4. **Limit Caffeine and Sugar:** Avoid sugary snacks or caffeinated beverages in the afternoon and evening, as they can disrupt sleep.

Physical Activity: A Natural Mood Regulator

Physical activity is one of the most effective tools for reducing stress, improving mood, and managing impulsivity—factors that directly influence ODD behaviors. Exercise helps regulate neurotransmitters like serotonin and dopamine, which are essential for emotional balance.

Example Scenario

Sophia, a nine-year-old diagnosed with ODD, often had difficulty sitting still in class and would act out impulsively. Her parents incorporated more physical activity into her daily routine, scheduling 30 minutes of outdoor play in the morning and enrolling her in a dance class in the afternoons. The extra exercise provided Sophia with a constructive way to release her energy, significantly reducing her hyperactivity and disruptive behavior in the classroom.

Physical Activity Ideas for Children with ODD

1. **Outdoor Play**: Activities like running, biking, or playing soccer in the yard can provide an outlet for excess energy.
2. **Structured Sports:** Enroll your child in organized activities such as swimming, gymnastics, or martial arts to help with discipline and focus.

3. **Family Walks or Hikes:** A simple daily walk can be a great way to bond as a family while giving your child a chance to burn off energy and clear their mind.
4. **Indoor Movement Breaks:** For days when the weather doesn't allow for outdoor play, set up indoor obstacle courses or use yoga and stretching routines to help your child stay active and engaged.

The Role of Family Meal Routines in Behavior Management

Family meals are more than just an opportunity to ensure your child eats nutritious foods—they also provide a structured environment that promotes routine, communication, and emotional connection. Children with ODD often thrive on structure, and regular family meals can help strengthen cooperation and improve family dynamics.

Example Scenario

Liam's Mealtime Stability: Liam, a 10-year-old with ODD, often resisted sitting down for dinner, which led to arguments and tension in the household. His parents worked with a therapist to create a positive family meal routine. They set clear expectations around mealtime, encouraged Liam to help with small tasks like setting the table, and made family dinners screen-free to develop a better connection. By involving Liam in the process and making mealtimes predictable and positive, the family noticed a reduction in his defiant behavior during meals.

Strategies for Family Meals

1. **Establish Regular Meal Times:** Create a schedule where the family eats together at least once daily. This structure helps children know what to expect and gives them a sense of stability.
2. **Involve Your Child in Meal Prep:** Allow your child to help plan and prepare meals. Giving them responsibility and choice helps reduce defiance and encourages a sense of accomplishment.
3. **Make Meals a Relaxing, Device-Free Time:** Encourage conversation by making meals screen-free. Focus on connecting with your child and discussing positive topics to reduce stress and tension during meals.
4. **Use Mealtime for Positive Reinforcement:** Acknowledge and praise good behavior during meals, such as sitting quietly, helping with chores, or cooperating with siblings.

INTEGRATING DIET AND LIFESTYLE FOR COMPREHENSIVE ODD MANAGEMENT

While diet is critical in managing ODD, it is most effective when combined with other supportive lifestyle changes. Prioritizing sleep hygiene, encouraging regular physical activity, and establishing structured family routines can significantly improve emotional regulation and behavior in children with ODD. By adopting a holistic approach, parents can create a balanced and supportive environment that empowers their child to thrive physically and emotionally.

CHAPTER 8
THE ROLE OF PHYSICAL ACTIVITY IN MANAGING ODD

THE BENEFITS OF PHYSICAL ACTIVITY

Regular physical activity can be a game-changer for everyone. When your child engages in consistent exercise, it helps reduce stress, improve mood, and enhance overall mental well-being. Physical activity stimulates the production of endorphins, often referred to as "feel-good" hormones, which can alleviate anxiety and depression. Additionally, exercise promotes better sleep, which is vital for mood regulation and cognitive function. Incorporating physical activity into your child's routine creates a natural, effective way to manage some of the more challenging aspects of ODD.

Choosing the Right Physical Activity for Your Child

Finding the right type of physical activity for your child can make all the difference. The key is choosing activities that align with their interests and abilities. Team sports like soccer or basketball can be excellent for children who thrive on social interaction and enjoy teamwork. These sports provide physical exercise and teach valuable skills such as cooperation, communication, and discipline.

For children who may not enjoy team sports, individual activities like martial arts offer a structured environment that promotes self-discipline, focus, and physical fitness. Swimming is another fantastic option, combining the benefits of full-body exercise with the calming effects of water. Yoga can be particularly beneficial for children with ODD because it incorporates mindfulness and relaxation techniques alongside physical activity, which helps reduce stress and improve emotional regulation.

Integrating Physical Activity Into the Daily Routine

Integrating physical activity into your child's daily routine requires consistency. Begin by setting aside specific times each day dedicated to exercise. This might be a morning jog, an after-school sports practice, or an evening bike ride. The goal is to make physical activity a non-negotiable part of daily life, like brushing teeth or doing homework. Consistency is key because it reinforces the habit, making it a regular and expected part of your child's day. Begin with small, manageable increments and gradually increase the duration as your child becomes more accustomed to the routine. For example, start with a 10-minute walk around the neighborhood and gradually extend it to a 30-minute run. Integrating these activities into your daily schedule ensures they become a natural part of your child's life.

Overcoming Resistance to Exercise

Encouraging a child who resists exercise can be challenging, but some strategies can help. Start by making the activities fun and engaging. Choose exercises your child enjoys, and consider incorporating games or challenges to keep things interesting. Setting achievable goals can also motivate your child. For instance, you could create a reward system where they earn points for each completed activity that can be exchanged for a reward they value, such as going to a movie or a special outing. Another practical approach is participating in the activities with your child because this provides encouragement and support and turns exercise into a bonding opportunity. If your child sees you enjoying the activity, they are likelier to join in and have fun.

Creative Ways to Encourage Physical Activity

Let's consider a scenario where your child strongly resists physical activity. One approach could be to start with something straightforward and appealing, like a family dance party in the living room. Play their favorite music and let loose together. The key is to make it feel less like exercise and more like play. Gradually, you can introduce more structured activities. For example, if your child enjoys video games, consider active games requiring physical movement. These can be a gateway to more traditional forms of exercise. Additionally, involving your child in choosing the activities can give them a sense of control and investment and make them more likely to participate willingly.

Regular physical activity is a powerful tool in managing ODD symptoms, offering numerous benefits from reduced stress to improved mood. By selecting suitable activities, ensuring consistency, and finding creative ways to overcome resistance, you can help your child incorporate exercise into their routine. This supports their physical health and contributes significantly to their emotional and behavioral well-being.

STRUCTURING A HOME ENVIRONMENT CONDUCIVE TO WELL-BEING

Creating a well-structured home environment plays an essential role in reducing stress, promoting emotional regulation, and preparing the foundation for healthy physical activity. When children feel calm and supported in their surroundings, they are more likely to engage in positive activities, including exercise, which is vital for managing ODD. A clutter-free, organized, and balanced environment can encourage movement, play, and active engagement, leading naturally into physical activity routines. This connection between calming home space and active play will help your child establish mental and physical balance, which will be explored further in the next section.

The Role of Clutter-Free Environments

A clutter-free environment is particularly important for children with ODD. Minimizing clutter reduces overstimulation and provides a sense of order, positively affecting your child's ability to manage stress. Use storage bins and shelves to neatly arrange toys, books, and other items. This fosters a sense of control over their surroundings and minimizes potential distractions that could lead to irritability or defiant behaviors. Having clearly defined spaces for different activities, like a homework station or a play area, encourages a smoother flow of the day and helps your child feel more grounded.

For further insights on how clutter impacts children's stress levels, you might want to explore the growing field of environmental psychology. Studies suggest an organized space can support better focus and emotional regulation, especially in children with behavioral challenges.

Using Colors to Promote Calm and Balance

Using specific colors and decor can significantly influence your child's mood and behavior. Bright, bold colors may stimulate and sometimes exacerbate feelings of restlessness or irritability. Instead, choose soothing colors like soft blues, greens, and neutrals that are calming. Research in color psychology shows that these cooler tones help reduce anxiety and encourage relaxation. You can also incorporate elements from nature, such as potted plants or nature-themed artwork, to create a calming, grounded environment. Minimize visual clutter by keeping the decor simple and organized.

Research papers on color psychology and its impact on children with behavioral disorders are useful for a more in-depth understanding. These studies explore how certain color schemes in classrooms and homes affect children's emotional responses and behaviors, providing additional evidence that the right color choices can make a difference (neurolaunch.com).

Establishing Routines and Clear Rules

Establishing consistent routines and clear rules can help children with ODD feel secure and understand expectations. When daily activities follow a predictable pattern, it reduces anxiety and uncertainty, which can trigger defiant behaviors. Create a visual schedule on a large calendar that outlines the day's activities, including wake-

THE ROLE OF PHYSICAL ACTIVITY IN MANAGING ODD

up time, meals, school, playtime, and bedtime. Clear rules should be simple and easy to understand, with consistent enforcement. This stability reinforces positive behaviors and reduces the likelihood of conflicts.

To explore the impact of routine on behavioral regulation more deeply, you can explore studies that emphasize the importance of structured environments for children with ODD and other behavioral challenges.

Incorporating Sensory Tools for Emotional Regulation

Incorporating sensory tools into your home environment can support your child's ability to self-regulate emotions and behaviors. Sensory tools like stress balls, weighted blankets, or fidget spinners can provide physical outlets for frustration or anxiety. A sensory corner with various tools lets your child choose what works best for them. Background music, mainly instrumental or nature sounds, can also create a calming atmosphere and reduce anxiety.

For further reading, you can explore sensory integration therapy resources or articles on how sensory tools can aid emotional regulation for children with behavioral challenges.

A Day in a Structured, Supportive Environment

Imagine your child coming home from a challenging day at school. They walk into a calm, organized home where they know exactly where to find their favorite book and can retreat to a cozy corner with a weighted blanket. The soothing colors on the walls and the soft music playing in the background further help them unwind. They follow a familiar routine: a snack, some quiet playtime, and then starting on their homework. The precise rules and consistent schedule provide a sense of stability and security. If they feel overwhelmed, they reach for a stress ball from their sensory corner and find relief in the tactile stimulation. This structured and supportive environment can make a significant difference in managing their ODD symptoms, promoting a sense of well-being and balance.

Creating a home environment conducive to well-being involves thoughtful organization, mindful use of colors and decor, consistent routines, clear rules, and the incorporation of sensory tools. These elements work together to create a space where your child feels secure, understood, and supported, helping reduce behavioral issues and improve overall emotional health. This structured environment also paves the way for healthy physical activity and fosters a balanced mental and physical well-being approach.

For more guidance, consider reading books or research papers on the impact of environment and routine on children with behavioral challenges. These resources can provide further insight into how subtle changes in the home environment can lead to significant improvements in emotional regulation and behavior.

THE INFLUENCE OF SCREEN TIME AND DIGITAL DEVICES

Managing screen time is essential in promoting healthy physical activity and well-being in children. Creating a balance between screen use and physical activity can be major for overall development. As we dive into the role of screens, it's important to recognize how this balance supports a holistic approach to behavior management and emotional regulation, leading to the need for physical activity.

The Impact of Excessive Screen Time

In today's digital age, screens are an inevitable part of your child's life. However, the time spent on these devices can significantly affect behavior and overall well-being. Current recommendations suggest that children six and older should have no more than two hours of recreational screen time daily. For younger children, the limit should be even lower. Excessive screen time can lead to several adverse effects, including increased irritability, difficulty concentrating, and disrupted sleep patterns. When children spend too much time on screens, it can interfere with their ability to wind down at night, which leads to poor sleep quality and exacerbates behavioral issues.

Research on Screen Time and Emotional Regulation

Research indicates that early tablet use in young children is associated with increased expressions of anger and frustration as they age. A study published in *JAMA Pediatrics* followed children from the ages of 3.5 to 5.5 years and found that higher levels of tablet use at 3.5 years were linked to more frequent and intense expressions of anger and frustration by the age of 4.5 (Fitzpatrick et al., 2023). This study suggests a bidirectional relationship where increased tablet use can lead to heightened emotional outbursts, and in turn, these outbursts may lead to more tablet use over time. The result highlights the importance of monitoring and managing screen time to mitigate potential negative impacts on emotional regulation in young children.

Balancing Screen Time with Physical and Cognitive Activities

Balancing screen time with other activities is important for promoting a well-rounded development in your child. Encourage physical, social, and cognitive activities that provide enriching experiences away from screens. For example, schedule regular family outings like hiking or trips to the park, which offer physical exercise and opportunities for social interaction. Board games and puzzles can stimulate cognitive development and encourage family bonding. Arts and crafts sessions can unleash creativity and provide a constructive outlet for your child's energy. Creating a balanced mix of activities helps your child develop various skills and reduce the over-reliance on digital devices.

The Importance of Content Quality

The type of content your child engages with on screens also matters significantly. Educational content can be beneficial by providing opportunities for learning and cognitive development. Programs that teach math, science, or reading skills can supplement your child's education. However, entertainment content, especially violent or aggressive media, can negatively impact behavior, making children more prone to aggression and defiance. Monitoring the type of content and encouraging educational over purely entertaining media can mitigate some of the negative impacts of screen time. For instance, interactive educational games can be engaging and informative, balancing fun and learning.

Setting Guidelines for Healthy Screen Use

Effectively managing and monitoring your child's screen use involves setting clear guidelines and creating a supportive environment. Start by establishing "technology-free" times and zones within your home. For instance, designate meal times and the hour before bed as relaxing screen-free periods. Create zones, such as the dining room and bedrooms, where screens are not allowed. This helps reinforce the importance of face-to-face interactions and ensures that screen time does not interfere with sleep. Setting up parental controls on devices can also be beneficial. These controls allow you to monitor the types of content your child accesses and limit their screen time. To make enforcing these guidelines easier, many devices have built-in features that let you set daily time limits and block inappropriate content.

A Real-Life Example of Screen Time Management

Consider a family who struggled with their child's excessive screen time. They noticed increased irritability and trouble sleeping. By establishing screen-free times and monitoring content, they saw a marked improvement in their child's behavior and sleep quality. They started by making dinner time a screen-free zone, encouraging conversation and family bonding. They also set up parental controls to limit access to certain types of content and enforced a strict no-screen policy an hour before bedtime. This structured approach reduced screen time and helped the child develop healthier habits and routines, improving overall behavior and well-being.

In summary, managing screen time and digital device use is critical to supporting your child with ODD. By adhering to recommended guidelines, balancing screen time with other enriching activities, monitoring content, and setting clear boundaries, you can help mitigate the adverse effects of excessive screen use. Doing so creates space for healthier habits, such as physical activity and social interaction, which are integral to their overall well-being.

RESEARCH STUDIES ON SCHOOL-BASED PHYSICAL ACTIVITY PROGRAMS AND ODD

Physical activity is a powerful tool for improving attention, mood, and overall behavior in children with ODD. Regular exercise stimulates the production of endorphins, which are natural mood enhancers, reducing anxiety and promoting a sense of well-being. This boost in mood can lead to better emotional regulation and a decrease in oppositional behaviors. Moreover, physical activity enhances cognitive function by improving attention and focus, making it easier for children with ODD to manage tasks and follow instructions.

Studies have shown that school-based physical activity programs can significantly improve student behavior and reduce disciplinary issues. These programs provide structured opportunities for children to exercise, which helps channel their energy constructively and decreases the likelihood of disruptive behavior. Additionally, the social aspects of these activities, such as teamwork and communication, contribute to better behavioral control and improved interactions with peers and teachers.

Incorporating regular physical activity into children's daily routine supports their overall physical health and helps manage symptoms, leading to more balanced and positive behavior overall.

EXAMPLES OF PHYSICAL ACTIVITIES FOR CHILDREN WITH ODD

1. Aerobic Exercises

Running or Jogging: Encourage short runs or jogs, which can be done in a park or around the neighborhood.

Cycling: Bike rides can be both enjoyable and a great way to get aerobic exercise.

2. Team Sports

Soccer: Promotes teamwork, coordination, and cardiovascular fitness.

Basketball: Enhances hand-eye coordination, teamwork, and physical endurance.

3. Individual Sports

Swimming: Provides a great full-body workout and can be calming.

Martial Arts: Improves discipline, focus, and self-control.

4. Outdoor Activities

Hiking: Combines physical activity with the calming effects of nature.

Playing at the Park: Engages in various forms of play and social interaction.

5. Structured Exercise Programs

Dance Classes: Fun way to improve coordination and physical fitness.

Gymnastics: Builds strength, flexibility, and discipline.

6. Mind-Body Activities

Yoga: Enhances flexibility, strength, and mindfulness, helping with emotional regulation.

Tai Chi: Combines gentle physical activity with mindfulness and relaxation techniques.

7. Recreational Activities

Trampoline: Fun way to improve cardiovascular health and coordination.

Skating: Rollerblading or ice skating improves balance and fitness.

INTEGRATING PHYSICAL ACTIVITY INTO DAILY ROUTINE

Engaging in regular physical activities as a family provides support and encouragement, helping children stay motivated and active. Consistency, such as daily walks or weekend sports, reinforces healthy habits, while adding variety keeps activities enjoyable and engaging. Using positive reinforcement, like celebrating achievements, further encourages participation and builds confidence.

Regular physical activity can significantly improve symptoms of ODD in children by enhancing mood, reducing stress, and improving behavior. Integrating various enjoyable physical activities into the child's daily routine can provide both physical and mental health benefits, contributing to overall well-being and better management of ODD symptoms.

For children with ODD who are beginners or dislike physical activity, introduce physical activities in a fun, engaging, and non-intimidating way. Here are some suggestions that can help.

BEGINNER-FRIENDLY PHYSICAL ACTIVITIES

1. Walking

Walking is easy to start, gentle on the body, and can be done anywhere. To keep it engaging, try turning walks into nature scavenger hunts, exploring new parks, or taking along a pet for added fun.

2. Dancing

Dancing is enjoyable, improves coordination, and boosts cardiovascular health. To make it even more exciting, play favorite songs for a dance-off or follow along with dance videos or interactive games like *Just Dance*.

3. Yoga

Yoga enhances flexibility, balance, and mindfulness. Make it enjoyable for kids with yoga videos or apps that incorporate storytelling and fun poses inspired by animals or superheroes.

4. Biking

Biking is a great cardiovascular exercise that can be enjoyed at a relaxed pace. Make it more exciting by biking together as a family, exploring new trails, or creating a simple obstacle course in a safe area.

5. Swimming

Swimming offers a full-body, low-impact workout that often feels like play. Make it more enjoyable by playing pool games like Marco Polo, organizing a relay race, or simply allowing for free swim time.

CREATING FUN AND ENGAGING PHYSICAL ACTIVITIES

1. Hula Hooping

Hula hooping improves core strength and coordination, and it's easy to make it enjoyable with hula hoop contests or by learning new tricks together.

2. Trampoline

Jumping is excellent for cardiovascular health and strengthens the legs. Make it more enjoyable by jumping on a mini-trampoline while listening to music or playing games like "Simon Says" with jumping commands.

3. Obstacle Courses

Creating a simple obstacle course with household items like pillows, chairs, and ropes can make an engaging activity that enhances agility, strength, and problem-solving skills. Set it up in your backyard or home for a fun challenge.

4. Playground Activities

Playgrounds promote physical activity through climbing, swinging, and sliding. Make visits more engaging by exploring different playgrounds, joining in on the fun, and encouraging creative play.

5. Ball Games

Playing games like catch, soccer, four square, or dodgeball improves hand-eye coordination and social skills while keeping the activity fun and engaging.

Case Study 1: Jackson's Journey to Teamwork and Cooperation Through Soccer

Jackson, a 10-year-old boy diagnosed with ODD, often struggled with defiance and impulsivity, particularly at school. His parents decided to enroll him in a soccer program, hoping that the structure and teamwork involved in the sport would help channel his energy positively. Initially, Jackson was resistant, finding it difficult to follow the rules and cooperate with his teammates. However, his coach was patient and used a reward system to encourage effort rather than results.

After a few weeks, Jackson began to enjoy soccer and developed a sense of pride in being part of a team. His parents noticed significant improvements in his behavior on and off the field. He started to listen more attentively and was more cooperative with his teachers and classmates. Soccer provided Jackson with a physical outlet for his energy and taught him valuable lessons about discipline, teamwork, and communication, which helped him manage his ODD symptoms.

Case Study 2: Emma Finds Calm Through Yoga

Emma, an eight-year-old girl with ODD, had frequent emotional outbursts and found it challenging to regulate her emotions. Traditional team sports did not appeal to her, so her mother introduced her to a kids' yoga class. Emma was initially skeptical, but the class incorporated storytelling and animal-themed yoga poses, which caught her attention.

Over time, Emma started looking forward to her yoga sessions. She began using breathing techniques and mindfulness exercises from yoga to calm herself when frustrated. Her teacher noticed that Emma could better focus and control her reactions during class, and her parents reported fewer emotional outbursts at home. Yoga became a calming, enjoyable part of her routine that allowed her to manage her emotions more effectively.

Case Study 3: Ryan's Transformation Through Martial Arts

Ryan, a 12-year-old with ODD, was known for his defiance and difficulty following rules. His parents decided to try martial arts to channel his energy into something structured but empowering. Martial arts provided Ryan with physical activity, discipline, and goal-setting. The belt-ranking system gave him clear, achievable milestones to work toward, which helped motivate him.

At first, Ryan struggled with the strict rules of martial arts, but as he progressed, he began enjoying the structure and focus it required. The physical activity helped him manage his impulsivity, and the lessons in self-discipline carried over into his daily life. Over time, Ryan became more respectful of authority in his martial arts class and school, significantly improving his behavior.

Case Study 4: Sarah's Family Hiking Adventures

Sarah, a nine-year-old girl with ODD, often became overwhelmed by large groups and structured team sports. Her parents wanted to find a form of physical activity that could allow Sarah to unwind while giving her a sense of accomplishment. They decided to make hiking a family tradition on the weekends. At first, Sarah was reluctant, but they made the hikes fun by incorporating scavenger hunts and nature exploration.

Sarah began to enjoy the peacefulness of nature, and hiking provided her with an outlet to release her energy in a calm environment. The regular family hikes also helped strengthen their bond, as they spent quality time together without the distractions of technology or external stressors. Over time, Sarah's behavior at home and school improved as the physical activity and family connection helped her manage her ODD symptoms more effectively.

ENGAGING ACTIVITIES THAT FEEL LIKE PLAY

1. Interactive Video Games

Combining screen time with physical activity can be engaging and fun through games that require movement, like Wii Sports, Ring Fit Adventure, or Just Dance. These interactive games make it easy to stay active while enjoying screen time.

2. Treasure Hunts

Encouraging walking, running, and problem-solving, a treasure hunt can be made fun by creating a simple map and hiding small toys or treats around the house or yard for children to find.

3. Creative Movement Games

Activities that encourage both movement and creativity, like Freeze Dance—where children dance until the music stops—and Animal Walks, where they mimic different animals, make staying active enjoyable and imaginative.

4. Gardening

Gardening offers light physical activity that is calming and rewarding. Make it enjoyable by planting flowers and vegetables together or creating a small herb garden.

5. DIY Sports

Introducing sports in a non-competitive way can be fun and engaging with simple activities like bowling using plastic bottles, mini-golf with household items, or a homemade ring toss. These activities encourage participation without pressure.

TIPS FOR ENCOURAGING PARTICIPATION

To encourage physical activity, try tying activities to the child's interests, like dancing to favorite songs or exploring intriguing places. Use positive reinforcement with praise and rewards to celebrate participation and achievements, no matter how small. Start with short, manageable sessions and gradually increase the duration as the child gains comfort. Family involvement can make activities more enjoyable, and allowing the child to choose or offering alternative options when they resist helps keep things flexible and engaging.

Incorporating physical activity into children's daily lives with behavioral challenges offers immediate benefits like mood regulation, stress reduction, and long-lasting mental health advantages extending into adulthood. These findings underscore the importance of including structured physical activities, such as team sports or other consistent physical routines, as a holistic strategy to manage behavioral issues.

As we conclude this chapter, it's evident that exercise and lifestyle choices play a significant role in managing ODD symptoms. Each element contributes to a holistic approach to improving your child's behavior and emotional health, from physical activity and promoting overall well-being to creating a supportive home environment and managing screen time.

CHAPTER 9
SELF-CARE FOR PARENTS

Parenting a child with ODD is a journey that demands immense emotional strength, patience, and perseverance. Often, in the whirlwind of managing challenging behaviors and daily responsibilities, parents overlook their own needs. This chapter is dedicated to you—the parent who gives so much, sometimes at the expense of your well-being.

Self-care is not a luxury; it is necessary to sustain your ability to be the best parent you can be. Prioritizing your mental and emotional health will improve your resilience and create a healthier environment for your child. Through strategies for managing stress, recognizing burnout, and building a strong support network, this chapter provides tools to help you rediscover balance, strength, and hope. You deserve to care for yourself just as you care for your child, and this chapter will guide you in finding that path.

In addition to the self-care strategies outlined here, creating a support network for yourself is important. Surrounding yourself with family, friends, or community resources will strengthen your ability to manage stress. Chapter 10 will offer further insights into managing ODD-specific challenges, giving you a comprehensive toolkit for navigating your parenting journey.

RECOGNIZING SIGNS OF PARENTAL BURNOUT

Burnout often begins with intense, unshakable fatigue. Emotional detachment and irritability may creep in, turning minor issues into major frustrations. This exhaustion can erode one's sense of accomplishment and lead to feelings of inadequacy. The lack of a solid support system and societal pressures worsen this isolation. Recognizing these signs early is key.

Self-assessment tools, like checklists and journaling, can help monitor your emotional state. These tools provide insight into triggers and stressors, allowing you to address them proactively.

Self-Assessment Checklist: Recognizing Parental Burnout

- Are you feeling drained most of the time?
- Are you more easily frustrated or angered?
- Do you feel disconnected from loved ones?
- Do you often feel ineffective as a parent?
- Are you experiencing frequent mood swings?
- Are you struggling with sleep?
- Are you experiencing physical symptoms like headaches or stomach issues?

Acknowledging the need for help is a courageous step. Seeking support from friends, family, or professionals shows strength and commitment to being your best parent.

STRATEGIES FOR MANAGING PARENTAL STRESS

Managing stress requires a multifaceted approach. Incorporate mindfulness meditation and relaxation exercises into your daily routine to create a sense of calm. Journaling can help untangle emotions and offer new perspectives. Even a few minutes of physical activity can clear your mind and lift your spirits. Set realistic goals to avoid frustration and recognize that progress, not perfection, is the aim.

Delegate tasks within the household or seek external help to lighten your load, reducing stress while empowering others to contribute. Incorporate daily gratitude practices, like noting positives, to shift focus from stress to small victories and joys.

Case Study: Discovering a Gratifying Self-Nurturing Routine

Megan, the mother of 11-year-old Ethan, had been struggling to manage her stress while dealing with the challenges of his ODD. Ethan's frequent outbursts and defiance left her feeling drained, both emotionally and physically. She often felt overwhelmed, and her frustration was affecting her relationship with her son and her overall outlook on life.

One day, Megan decided to try something different after a particularly difficult week. She remembered reading about the importance of self-care and stress management, so she set out to create a self-nurturing routine. She began each morning with 10 minutes of mindfulness meditation, focusing on breathing exercises to center herself before the day began. At first, it felt foreign, but over time, she noticed that this simple practice gave her a sense of calm and clarity throughout the day.

Megan also incorporated daily journaling into her routine, setting aside 15 minutes in the evening to reflect on her emotions. Writing about her frustrations, challenges, and small wins helped her untangle the intense emotions she had bottled up. She also started jotting down three things she was grateful for each day, shifting her focus from the overwhelming stress to the positive moments, no matter how small.

Realizing the importance of physical activity, Megan also began taking short evening walks in her neighborhood. These walks provided her with fresh air and a mental break, lifted her spirits, and helped her release built-up tension.

As Megan's routine became more ingrained, she noticed a significant change in her outlook. The combination of mindfulness, journaling, gratitude practices, and physical activity gave her a renewed sense of balance. She was better equipped to handle Ethan's outbursts without feeling emotionally depleted. Instead of focusing solely on the difficult moments, she found herself appreciating Ethan's progress, however small it might be. She also started delegating tasks at home by encouraging her older daughter and husband to take on more responsibilities, which lightened her load.

Megan's self-nurturing routine became a source of strength and resilience. By prioritizing her well-being, she improved her relationship with Ethan and rediscovered a sense of joy and positivity in her everyday life.

BUILDING A SUPPORT NETWORK: FINDING AND USING RESOURCES

A strong support network is essential. Identify immediate sources of support—family, friends, or community groups. Explore professional options like therapists specializing in ODD. Online communities and virtual support groups offer a lifeline for sharing experiences and gaining advice. Creating a personal support plan helps maintain these connections and ensures you have the emotional and practical support needed. Maintain social connections beyond your support network, such as friends or interest-based groups, to prevent isolation and enhance your well-being.

Case Study: Finding Connection and Support Through an Online Group

Danielle, a single mother of nine-year-old Lucas, had been struggling to cope with the demands of parenting her child with ODD. Danielle was left feeling isolated and unsure of her parenting choices. Most of her friends and family didn't fully understand the complexities of Lucas's behavior, and Danielle often felt like she had no one to turn to for advice or emotional support.

In search of help, Danielle joined an online support group for parents of children with ODD. Initially, she was hesitant to share her experiences, but after reading posts from other parents going through similar struggles, she felt relief. For the first time, she wasn't alone. The group quickly became a lifeline for her.

Danielle began actively participating in discussions, asking for advice, and offering support to others. She connected with a few members who had older children with ODD and learned from their experiences. One of the group members, Michelle, who lived in a different state, became a particularly close friend. They shared weekly updates on their children's progress, discussing new techniques they were trying, such as reward systems and collaborative problem-solving approaches. These conversations gave Danielle practical tools to manage Lucas's behavior and provided her with much-needed emotional support.

Over time, Danielle developed lasting friendships with several other group members. They started a smaller, private chat where they could have more in-depth conversations and check in on one another regularly. These long-term connections gave Danielle the strength to navigate the day-to-day challenges of parenting Lucas. She no longer felt isolated and knew she had a network of people who truly understood her journey.

The support Danielle found online also inspired her to branch out socially. Encouraged by her newfound confidence, she joined a local book club to engage with other adults on topics unrelated to parenting. This helped her maintain balance and gave her a break from the constant focus on Lucas's ODD and allowing her to develop a well-rounded support system.

In the end, the online support group was a community that empowered Danielle to manage the challenges of ODD with greater resilience. The long-term connections she made helped her feel supported, validated, and hopeful about her ability to provide Lucas with the guidance he needed.

BUILDING A SUPPORT NETWORK FOR PARENTS

There are several well-established online forums, support groups, and therapy programs that can offer guidance and community support for parents of children diagnosed with ODD. These resources provide educational materials, emotional support, and practical advice.

1. **Oppositional Defiant Disorder Support Group on Facebook**
    - **Website:** https://www.facebook.com/groups/oddsupport
    - **Description:** This is a large, active group where parents share personal experiences, tips, and emotional support related to raising children with ODD. It offers real-time discussions with other parents in similar situations.
    - **Support:** The group provides a safe place to ask questions and share strategies for managing ODD at home.
2. **ADDitude Magazine Community Forums**
    - **Website:** https://www.additudemag.com/forums/
    - **Description:** ADDitude offers a range of resources for ADHD and related conditions, including ODD. Their forums allow parents to discuss behavioral management, discipline techniques, and coping strategies.
    - **Support:** The forums are active with parents and experts sharing experiences and providing guidance on managing children with ODD.

Your mental health is the cornerstone of effective parenting. Recognize signs of struggle early, and don't hesitate to seek professional help. Regular self-reflection, mindfulness, and therapeutic activities are vital to maintaining your well-being and ensuring a supportive environment for you and your child.

Caring for a child with ODD is no easy feat, but through the challenges, you are building a foundation of strength, resilience, and love. By nurturing yourself, you ensure you are better equipped to meet your child's needs with patience and compassion. The journey can feel overwhelming at times, but small, meaningful changes in how you care for yourself can significantly improve your outlook and well-being.

Remember, you are not alone in this process. As you build a support network and integrate self-care into your routine, you will find strength in both community and personal growth. Every moment of mindfulness, connection with another parent, and step toward your well-being move you closer to a future filled with hope and possibility.

Parenting a child with ODD may bring unpredictable challenges, but it also presents opportunities for deeper understanding, stronger relationships, and personal resilience. With the right tools, support, and perspective, you can navigate this path and find joy, fulfillment, and optimism for you and your child. Keep moving forward—you are stronger than you know, and hope is always ahead.

CHAPTER 10
ADDRESSING COMMON QUESTIONS AND CONCERNS

Parenting a child with ODD presents unique challenges that can often feel overwhelming, especially when progress seems slow or elusive. Many parents wonder if they're doing enough or taking the proper steps. This chapter is designed to address the most common questions and concerns parents of children with ODD face. It offers practical strategies, real-world case studies, and thoughtful advice to guide you through difficult moments.

You are not alone in this journey, and it's important to remember that your efforts, even when nothing is working, are making a difference. The key is to stay flexible, open to new ideas, and willing to adjust your strategies as your child grows and develops. Through patience, persistence, and support, you can help your child navigate their challenges and strengthen your resilience.

"WHAT IF I'VE TRIED EVERYTHING?": ADDRESSING DESPAIR

When it seems like nothing is working, start by acknowledging your frustration—this is a natural response to the complex challenges of ODD. Prioritize self-care to maintain your well-being during these moments. Explore alternative therapies like neurofeedback or equine-assisted therapy, and regularly re-evaluate your child's condition with professionals. Tracking progress and setbacks can provide valuable insights and help adjust strategies, and seeking second opinions can also offer new perspectives. Staying flexible and open to different approaches is critical to managing ODD effectively.

Case Study: Finding New Perspectives Through Second Opinions

Sarah, the mother of an eight-year-old boy named Stefan, struggled for years to find a solution for his ODD. Stefan's behavior had grown increasingly disruptive at home and school despite Sarah following advice from their primary pediatrician and behavioral therapist. The techniques they suggested—such as reward systems and strict consequences—seemed to have little effect. Stefan continued to lash out, and Sarah found herself emotionally drained and on the verge of despair.

Feeling that she had exhausted all options, Sarah sought a second opinion from a different specialist. The new pediatric psychiatrist suggested a more holistic approach, incorporating mindfulness techniques and involving Stefan in structured physical activities like martial arts to help him channel his energy and frustration more productively. They also recommended trying neurofeedback, a therapy Sarah had never considered.

Though hesitant at first, Sarah remained open to these new ideas. Over time, Stefan started showing gradual improvements. His episodes of defiance became less frequent, and he began expressing his feelings more calmly. The psychiatrist emphasized the importance of ongoing flexibility, encouraging Sarah to adapt her approach as Stefan grew and developed.

This experience underscored to Sarah the value of staying open to new perspectives. Had she not sought a second opinion, she might have relied on ineffective methods and prolonged her and Stefan's struggle. Additionally, her willingness to remain flexible and adjust her strategies based on Stefan's evolving needs became a cornerstone of her approach to parenting.

MANAGING JUDGMENT FROM OUTSIDERS

It's common to feel judged by others who don't understand ODD. To help mitigate this judgement, build confidence in your parenting decisions by trusting your knowledge and experience. Prepare responses to unsolicited advice, such as, "We're working with professionals on a plan that suits our child's needs." Educate friends and family about ODD to provide understanding and connect with support networks for validation and shared experiences. Remember to practice self-care to handle judgment and maintain your resilience.

Case Study: Responding Tactfully to Judgment from Outsiders

Jessica, the mother of 10-year-old Richard, often received unsolicited advice and judgment from family members and other parents who didn't understand her son's ODD. Jessica's mother-in-law frequently commented at family gatherings, "If you were just stricter with him, this wouldn't be a problem," or "Back in my day, kids weren't allowed to behave like this." These remarks made Jessica feel unsupported and defensive, and she often left the conversations feeling hurt.

Determined to manage the situation more effectively, Jessica developed a more tactful approach. She consulted her therapist, who helped her develop calm, confident responses to address the judgment while setting clear boundaries. The next time her mother-in-law made a critical comment, Jessica responded, "I understand that you have different views on discipline, but we're working with professionals on a plan tailored to Richard's specific needs. We've seen some progress and are committed to this approach."

Using this prepared response, Jessica could calmly assert her decisions without engaging in a defensive argument. Over time, her mother-in-law became less critical and even showed interest in learning more about ODD and Jessica's strategies. Jessica also found solace in joining an ODD support group where she connected with other parents facing similar challenges. Hearing their stories helped her feel less isolated and more confident in her parenting choices.

Through this process, Jessica learned that managing judgment from outsiders was about educating others and maintaining her well-being. By staying calm and focusing on her child's needs, she was able to handle criticism more effectively and build a more solid support network.

DISCERNING THE RIGHT TIME FOR PROFESSIONAL HELP

Recognizing when to seek professional help is essential. If your child's behaviors escalate or create significant distress within the family, it's time to consult with a pediatric psychiatrist, behavioral therapist, or family counselor. Collaborating with schools can also provide consistent support across environments. Prepare for consultations by documenting behaviors, gathering previous evaluations, and listing questions for the professional. This preparation helps ensure a productive session and a clear understanding of the next steps.

Case Study: Recognizing the Right Time for Professional Help

Emily, the mother of nine-year-old Michael, had been managing his ODD symptoms at home with basic behavioral techniques recommended by his pediatrician. These strategies—such as setting clear rules and rewarding positive behavior—seemed to keep things somewhat under control for a while. However, over the next year, Michael's behavior began to escalate. He became increasingly defiant and refused to follow instructions at home and school. His outbursts became more frequent and intense, and his younger sibling grew fearful of him.

Emily and her husband tried everything they could to manage the situation at home, but it became clear that Michael's behavior affected the entire family. They were constantly walking on eggshells, and the stress was starting to strain their relationship. Emily also noticed that Michael was struggling at school; his teacher reported that he had become disruptive and had difficulty focusing on his assignments. Despite their efforts, nothing seemed to be working anymore.

Realizing they could no longer handle the situation alone, Emily sought professional help. She started by consulting a pediatric psychiatrist who specialized in behavioral disorders like ODD. Before their appointment, Emily documented Michael's behaviors, noting specific incidents of defiance, aggression, and emotional outbursts. She also collected reports from his school and previous evaluations from his pediatrician. This thorough preparation allowed the psychiatrist to gain a clearer picture of Michael's condition.

The psychiatrist recommended a multifaceted approach, which included CBT for Michael and family counseling to help them navigate their roles in managing his behavior. The school was also brought into the loop, and they developed an IEP to support Michael's academic needs.

Looking back, Emily realized that seeking professional help was pivotal for their family. It provided much-needed support and helped them develop a more structured plan to address Michael's behavior. Involving professionals gave them new tools and strategies that improved Michael's behavior and the overall family dynamic.

ADJUSTING TECHNIQUES AS CHILDREN GROW

As your child grows, their needs and responses to strategies will change. Regularly review and revise behavior management techniques to keep them effective—tracking progress and setbacks will help you identify what works best. Involve your child in the process to give them a sense of ownership and responsibility. Stay informed on the latest developments in ODD management and discuss these with healthcare providers to refine your approach, and emphasize flexibility in your strategies to adapt to your child's evolving needs.

Case Study: Sophia's Journey to Shared Responsibility and Growth

Maria had been managing her daughter Sophia's ODD with a system of structured routines and reward-based behavior charts since she was six. For a few years, these methods worked well, helping Sophia understand her actions' expectations and consequences. However, as Sophia entered adolescence, Maria noticed these techniques were ineffective. Sophia began resisting the behavior charts, claiming they were "for little kids," and became more argumentative.

Maria recognized that it was time to adjust her approach. She consulted with Sophia's therapist, who suggested involving Sophia more actively in decision-making. Maria and Sophia sat down to revise the behavior management strategies, allowing Sophia to choose some of the rewards and consequences. This gave Sophia a sense of ownership over her behavior, and she responded positively to the increased responsibility. Maria also started tracking Sophia's progress with a journal, which helped them identify triggers for setbacks and moments of success.

As Sophia continued to grow, Maria remained flexible, involving healthcare professionals and regularly updating their approach to ensure it met Sophia's evolving needs.

OVERCOMING RESISTANCE TO CHANGE WITHIN THE FAMILY

Resistance to change is expected. Identify its sources and work toward a unified family approach to managing ODD. Regular family meetings help address concerns and ensure everyone is on the same page. If resistance persists, consider seeking support from a family therapist to navigate complex dynamics. Practicing flexibility and self-care can also reduce resistance and build a supportive family environment.

Case Study: Overcoming Resistance in the Johnson Family

Only some were on board when the Johnson family began implementing new strategies for managing their son Alex's ODD. Alex's older brother, Mark, resented the extra attention Alex received and felt that the family's routines were being disrupted. Meanwhile, Alex's father, David, was skeptical of the changes, believing stricter discipline would be more effective.

Recognizing the tension, Sarah, Alex's mother, organized regular family meetings to address the concerns and open communication. These meetings became a safe space for everyone to express their feelings. With the help of a family therapist, they could discuss how resistance was affecting their efforts to support Alex. David and Mark began to understand that the new strategies weren't about excusing Alex's behavior but helping him learn to manage it more effectively.

Working through their resistance as a family made them more unified in their approach. With everyone on the same page, they saw improvements in both Alex's behavior and the overall family dynamic.

DEALING WITH THE STIGMA OF MEDICATION

Misconceptions about medication can create unnecessary stigma. Understand that medication is a tool to help manage ODD, not a sign of failure. Discuss the pros and cons with healthcare providers and closely monitor your child's progress. Educate yourself and others about the role of medication in treatment to reduce stigma and build support. Track your child's medication response to ensure it effectively supports their needs.

Case Study: Emma's Journey to Overcome Medication Stigma

Emma was hesitant when her son, Thomas, was first prescribed medication for his ODD. She had grown up in a family where using medication for behavioral issues was stigmatized, and she feared that giving Thomas medication would be seen as a failure on her part as a parent. Her friends also voiced their concerns, warning her about potential side effects and labeling medication as a "last resort."

Emma decided to have an open discussion with Thomas's healthcare provider, who explained the role of medication in helping manage the more extreme aspects of his behavior. The doctor assured her that medication was one part of a broader treatment plan that included therapy and behavioral strategies. They also provided resources to educate Emma on the potential benefits and side effects.

After much consideration, Emma proceeded with the medication while closely monitoring Thomas's progress. She noticed an improvement in his ability to regulate his emotions, and their home life became less chaotic. Emma also tried to educate her family and friends about the decision, which helped reduce some of the stigma she had initially faced. Over time, she felt more confident in her choices and saw the medication as a helpful tool in managing Thomas's ODD.

STRATEGIES FOR SINGLE PARENTS MANAGING ODD

Single parents face unique challenges in managing ODD. To ease your burden, simplify behavior management strategies and build a strong support system, including family, friends, and community resources. Effective time management and self-care are essential to avoid burnout. Collaborating with schools can also provide additional support. Seek financial and legal assistance as needed.

Case Study: Managing ODD as a Single Parent—Jason's Story

Jason, a single father to seven-year-old Caleb, was overwhelmed by the demands of managing Caleb's ODD independently. Jason often felt burned out with a full-time job and no co-parent to share the responsibilities. Caleb's defiant behavior made mornings and evenings especially difficult, leaving Jason exhausted by the end of each day.

Jason simplified his behavior management strategies to ease the burden by focusing on just a few fundamental rules and rewards that Caleb could easily understand. He also contacted his parents and close friends and asked for help when he needed time to rest or focus on work. This support network became essential for Jason and allowed him to take breaks when needed.

Jason also collaborated with Caleb's school to ensure they followed the same behavior plan at home and in class. This consistency across environments made a significant difference in managing

Caleb's outbursts. Finally, Jason found a local support group for single parents of children with special needs where he gained advice and emotional support. With these strategies in place, Jason could better balance his well-being with his responsibilities as a parent.

ENSURING CONSISTENCY ACROSS DIFFERENT CAREGIVERS

Consistency across caregivers is important for effective ODD management. Communicate your child's care plan, provide written documentation, and hold regular updates with all caregivers. Training sessions for new caregivers can also ensure they're well-prepared to support your child. Flexibility in adapting the care plan as needed is essential for maintaining consistency across different environments.

Case Study: Ensuring Consistency for Jacob Across Caregivers

Lilian, the mother of six-year-old Jacob, noticed that his behavior would dramatically worsen whenever she left him in the care of his grandmother or babysitter. Despite making progress with Jacob's ODD at home, the lack of consistency between caregivers was setting him back. His grandmother tended to be lenient, while the babysitter had her approach, which led to confusion and frustration for Jacob.

Lilian realized that all caregivers needed to be on the same page for Jacob to succeed. She sat down with Jacob's grandmother, the babysitter, and the teacher to create a unified behavior management plan. Lilian provided written guidelines detailing the strategies for working at home and a chart for tracking Jacob's progress. They held regular check-ins to ensure everyone was following the same approach.

After creating a clear, consistent plan and involving all caregivers, Jacob began to show more stable behavior across different settings. The consistency gave him a sense of security, and over time, his outbursts diminished at home and when others were watching him.

Conclusion: Practical Strategies for Managing ODD

As you conclude this chapter, remember to focus on concrete, actionable steps to support you in your daily ODD management journey. Here are some key strategies you can implement immediately based on the insights shared.

- **Stay Open to New Approaches**: If you've tried everything, consider seeking alternative therapies like neurofeedback or structured physical activities such as martial arts. Regularly re-evaluating your child's progress with healthcare professionals can provide fresh perspectives and new solutions. Stay open to second opinions, especially when standard strategies aren't delivering results.
- **Manage External Judgment Proactively:** Develop prepared responses for unsolicited advice or criticism from others. By calmly asserting your parenting choices, such as stating, "We're working with professionals on a plan tailored to our child's needs," you can set boundaries and deflect negative judgment. Educating others about ODD and leaning on supportive networks can also help relieve external pressure.

- **Know When to Seek Professional Help:** Recognize when your child's behavior escalates beyond what you can manage at home. Consulting a pediatric psychiatrist, behavioral therapist, or counselor is critical when your family's well-being is at risk. Document your child's behavior, collect evaluations, and list key questions to ensure a productive professional consultation.
- **Adapt Strategies as Your Child Grows:** Your child's needs and responses to behavioral management will evolve. Review and revise strategies regularly, and involve your child when appropriate. Tracking their progress and setbacks will help you identify what's working and what needs adjusting. Flexibility is vital as your child matures.
- **Overcome Resistance in the Family:** Implement regular family meetings to encourage open communication about ODD management. If family members resist changes, consider seeking family therapy to help address concerns and align everyone with a unified approach. Flexibility and shared responsibility will help overcome resistance and create a supportive environment.
- **Address the Stigma of Medication**: If medication is part of your child's treatment plan, remember it's a tool to help manage symptoms, not a failure. Work closely with healthcare providers to monitor your child's progress and educate others to help reduce stigma. Stay informed and be confident in your choices, knowing that medication is one piece of a more extensive treatment puzzle.
- **Support for Single Parents:** Simplify behavior management strategies and build a strong support system of family, friends, and community resources. Collaborate with your child's school for consistent support across

environments, and don't hesitate to seek financial or legal assistance when needed.

- **Ensure Consistency Across Caregivers:** Clear communication with all caregivers is key for consistency. Provide written care plans, hold regular updates, and offer training sessions for new caregivers. This unified approach helps your child feel secure, knowing they're supported consistently across environments.

These practical steps, grounded in flexibility and adaptability, will help you better manage ODD while maintaining your well-being. Remember, progress may be gradual, but by staying proactive, seeking help when needed, and adjusting your strategies as your child grows, you are setting a path toward positive change for your child and your family. Stay strong, stay informed, and trust that each step forward—no matter how small—makes a difference.

CONCLUSION: A HOLISTIC APPROACH OF RESILIENCE, EMPATHY, AND ADVOCACY

As we close *The Oppositional Defiant Disorder Guide*, reflect on our journey marked by strategies, insights, and hope. Parenting a child with ODD is undoubtedly challenging, but you now possess the tools to navigate this path with empathy, patience, and resilience.

Throughout this book, we've explored evidence-based strategies for managing daily disruptions, enhancing communication, and fostering a supportive home environment. These approaches—behavior management, effective communication, and self-care—are the bedrock of creating a harmonious home. However, achieving long-term success requires a multifaceted approach, including proper nutrition, physical activity, and reducing screen time, which play equally significant roles in managing ODD symptoms.

Finding a good functional medicine practitioner is a key part of this journey. Such practitioners can offer valuable insights into addressing underlying nutritional deficiencies or imbalances contributing to your child's behavioral challenges. The right practitioner can guide you through personalized dietary plans, recommend supplements if necessary, and ensure that your child receives the nutrients needed for brain health and emotional regulation. Proper nutrition is the foundation for emotional and physical well-being, and integrating healthy eating habits into your child's life—as well as your own—can yield long-term benefits for the entire family.

Equally important is weaving in physical activity while limiting screen time. Regular exercise helps reduce stress and anxiety and promotes better sleep and emotional balance. Encouraging your child to engage in physical activities—whether through team sports, individual exercises like swimming or martial arts, or simple outdoor play—will enhance their mood and impulse control. Reducing screen time is essential, as excessive use of digital devices can lead to irritability, poor sleep, and an overstimulated mind. Balancing screen time with physical activities can help your child establish healthier habits that positively impact their overall behavior.

Remember, results take time. Changes in behavior and improvements in emotional regulation won't happen overnight. Patience and consistency are essential as you implement these strategies. Some days will be harder than others, and progress may seem slow at times, but each step forward—no matter how small—is a victory. Acknowledge and celebrate the incremental successes, as they are the building blocks of long-term progress.

Empathy for your child and yourself remains central to this journey. Recognize that your child's struggles are real, and your efforts to support them are invaluable. Equally important is prioritizing your well-being because taking care of yourself is essential. You are important, and your well-being matters.

The community around you—family, friends, and support networks—plays a vital role in this journey. Lean on them, share your experiences, and draw strength from their support. You are not alone; together, you can create an environment where your child can thrive.

Advocacy is another powerful tool at your disposal. Raising awareness and educating others about ODD contributes to a more inclusive and understanding society. Your efforts can help reduce stigma and pave the way for a better future for your child and others facing similar challenges.

Now, it's time to implement these strategies. Begin integrating them into your daily life. Progress may be gradual, but each step forward is a victory. Celebrate small successes, remain adaptable, and continue learning. This commitment to growth will keep you prepared and proactive throughout your journey.

Thank you for your unwavering dedication to supporting your child with ODD. Your commitment and resilience are commendable, and the positive impact of your efforts will resonate throughout your family's life. Every step you take makes a difference, and your efforts are deeply appreciated and recognized.

As you move forward, keep these lessons close to your heart. Approach each day with empathy, embrace continuous learning and adaptation, prioritize nutrition and physical activity, and advocate for your child's needs. Though challenging, this journey is filled with opportunities for growth, connection, and lasting positive change.

THANK YOU FOR READING!
YOUR REVIEW MATTERS

I hope "The Oppositional Defiant Disorder Guide" has brought you valuable insights and support throughout your journey. Now, I have a small favor to ask that could make a big impact.

If this book has been a helpful resource for you, would you take a moment to share your experience in a review?

Your feedback not only helps other parents find the guidance they need but also ensures that this book can reach more families looking for answers. A few words can go a long way in making a difference!

Thank you for your time and for being a part of this journey toward a more understanding and peaceful home.

Leave a review here:
https://www.amazon.com/review/create-review?asin=B0DMKCCZMM

With gratitude,
Michael Karl

REFERENCES

"4 Simple Ways to Jumpstart Clean Eating." n.d. Beth's Bountiful Bone Broth. https://simplyfinegourmet.com/blogs/health-diet/4-simple-way-to-jumpstart-clean-eating.

"18 Effective De-Escalation Strategies for Defusing Meltdowns." 2019. *Raising An Extraordinary Person* (blog). March 9, 2019. https://hes-extraordinary.com/de-escalation-techniques.

Aggarwal, Arpit, and Raman Marwaha. 2022. "Oppositional Defiant Disorder." In *StatPearls [Internet]*. StatPearls Publishing. https://www.ncbi.nlm.nih.gov/books/NBK557443/.

Bilici, M., Yildirim, F., Kandil, S., Bekaroglu, M., Yildirmis, S., Deger, O., Ulgen, M., Yildiran, A., and Aksu, H. "Double-Blind, Placebo-Controlled Study of Zinc Sulfate in the Treatment of Attention Deficit Hyperactivity Disorder." *Journal of Child and Adolescent Psychopharmacology* 14, no. 4 (2004): 555-562. https://doi.org/10.1089/cap.2004.14.555.

Battles, Magdalena. 2018. "10 Time Management Tips Every Busy Parent Needs to Know." *LifeHack* (blog). January 31, 2018. https://www.lifehack.org/663431/10-time-management-tips-every-busy-parent-needs-to-know.

Braaten, Ellen. 2021. "CBT Snapshot: Using Cognitive Behavior Therapy for Oppositional Defiant Disorder & Conduct Disorder." Clay Center for Young Healthy Minds. March 17, 2021. https://www.mghclaycenter.org/parenting-concerns/cbt-snapshot-using-cognitive-behavior-therapy-for-oppositional-defiant-disorder-conduct-disorder/.

"Breathwork Benefits for Your Mind, Body, and Soul." 2023. OneBreath Institute. September 6, 2023. https://www.onebreathinstitute.com/blog/breathwork-benefits-for-your-mind-body-and-soul.

"Building Strong Bonds: ODD Parenting Tips for Parents." n.d. BrightChamps. https://qltuh.cascaderange.top/space-robot/?pl=CHiI7Gh3GUyTa8XGgNqDyQ&sm=space-robot&click_id=cs6nhqt3kl6c73a2nsi0&nrid=b4c53d5287ac4c728fe5b7bbba62c3e6&hash=veAaJ1bs9IJuXykHZCTuNQ&exp=1728936471.

CDC. 2024. "Tips for Active Listening." Essentials for Parenting Toddlers and Preschoolers. August 8, 2024. https://www.cdc.gov/parenting-toddlers/communication/active-listening.html.

Chen, Zekun, Huanhuan Yang, Dongqing Wang, Christopher R. Sudfeld, Ai Zhao, Yiqian Xin, Jiawen Carmen Chen, Wafaie W. Fawzi, and Zhihui Li. "Effect of Oral Iron Supplementation on Cognitive Function among Children and Adolescents in

Low- and Middle-Income Countries: A Systematic Review and Meta-Analysis." *Nutrients* 14, no. 24 (2022): 5332. https://doi.org/10.3390/nu14245332.

"CPI's Top 10 de-Escalation Tips Revisited." 2022. Crisis Prevention Institute (CPI). June 28, 2022. https://www.crisisprevention.com/blog/general/cpi-s-top-10-de-escalation-tips-revisited/.

"Dealing with Adhd in Children: Part 2 – Healing with Exercises & Foods." 2023. Bhumi Sutra. May 16, 2023. https://bhumisutra.com/blogs/news/dealing-with-adhd-in-children-part-2-healing-with-exercises-foods.

Dewar, Gwen. 2020. "Parenting Stress: 12 Evidence-Based Tips for Making Life Better." PARENTING SCIENCE. November 14, 2020. https://parentingscience.com/parenting-stress-evidence-based-tips/.

———. 2024. "Teaching Empathy: Evidence-Based Tips." PARENTING SCIENCE. June 27, 2024. https://parentingscience.com/teaching-empathy-tips/.

Dieken, Caroline. 2005. "Oppositional Defiant Disorder: Using Family Therapy and Parent Training Techniques for Effective Treatment Outcomes Training Techniques for Effective Treatment Outcomes." University of Northern Iowa. https://scholarworks.uni.edu/cgi/viewcontent.cgi?article=1538&context=grp.

"Disability Rights." n.d. U.S. Department of Education. http://www.ed.gov/teaching-and-administration/safe-learning-environments/covid-19/disability-rights.

"Early Childhood Tablet Use Linked to Angry Outbursts." 2024. *American Psychiatric Association* (blog). August 16, 2024. https://alert.psychnews.org/2024/08/early-childhood-tablet-use-linked-to.html.

Eckart, Kim. 2018. "Practicing Mindfulness Benefits Parents and Children, UW Study Says." UW News (blog). September 25, 2018. https://www.washington.edu/news/2018/09/25/practicing-mindfulness-benefits-parents-and-children-uw-study-says/.

"Enhancing Cognitive Function: Key Supplements for Mental Sharpness and Memory." 2023. June 15, 2023. https://www.dietofcommonsense.com/enhancing-cognitive-function-key-supplements-for-mental-sharpness-and-memory/, https://www.dietofcommonsense.com/enhancing-cognitive-function-key-supplements-for-mental-sharpness-and-memory/.

"Evidence-Based Strategies for Oppositional Defiant Disorder (ODD)." n.d. NSW Government. https://education.nsw.gov.au/campaigns/inclusive-practice-hub/all-resources/secondary-resources/understanding-disability/oppositional-defiant-disorder/evidence-based-strategies.

Fitzpatrick, Caroline, et al. "Early-Childhood Tablet Use and Outbursts of Anger." *JAMA Pediatrics*, 2023. https://jamanetwork.com.

Frye, Devon. 2016. "Back from the Brink: Two Families' Stories of Oppositional Defiant Disorder." ADDitude (blog). November 2, 2016. https://www.additudemag.com/oppositional-defiant-disorder-adhd-family-stories/.

"Fun Ways to Incorporate Physical Activity into Daily Routines for Children with ADHD." 2023. Fatal Attraction. June 5, 2023. https://fatalatraction.com/23734-fun-ways-to-incorporate-physical-activity-into-daily-routines-for-children-with-adhd-09/.

Greydanus, Donald, and Catherine Dickson. 2022. "Oppositional Defiant and Conduct Disorders: Current Perspectives." *International Journal of Child Health and Human Development* 15, no. 4: 343–358. https://www.journalexample.com.

Hiser, Jaryd, and Michael Koenigs. 2018. "The Multifaceted Role of the Ventromedial Prefrontal Cortex in Emotion, Decision Making, Social Cognition, and Psychopathology." *Biological Psychiatry* 83 (8): 638–47. https://doi.org/10.1016/j.biopsych.2017.10.030.

Hosseini, Ebrahim. 2019. "Effectiveness of Social Skills Training on Reducing Symptoms of Oppositional Defiant Disorder in Children." Research Gate. May 2019. https://www.researchgate.net/publication/332933313_Effectiveness_of_social_skills_training_on_reducing_symptoms_of_oppositional_defiant_disorder_in_children.

"How to Eat Healthy & Feel Better: 8 Easy Steps." 2018. Sunwarrior. September 6, 2018. https://sunwarrior.com/blogs/health-hub/how-to-eat-healthy-feel-better-8-easy-steps.

Huberman, Andrew D. 2021. "Reducing Anxiety via the Physiological Sigh." *Stanford Medicine*. https://www.stanford.edu.

"IEP, 504 Plans: Navigating Special Services for Your Child." 2023. WRAL.Com. May 24, 2023. https://www.wral.com/story/iep-504-plans-navigating-special-services-for-your-child/20867785/.

Jafari, Niloufar, Mohammad Reza Mohammadi, Mehdi Khanbani, Saeedeh Farid, and Parisa Chiti. 2011. "Effect of Play Therapy on Behavioral Problems of Maladjusted Preschool Children." *Iranian Journal of Psychiatry* 6 (1): 37–42. https://www.ncbi.nlm.nih.gov/pmc/articles/PMC3395936/.

Jalal, Waseem. 2023. "Holistic Approaches to Adrenal Imbalance Treatment." August 3, 2023. https://statusaddiction.com/holistic-approaches-to-adrenal-imbalance-treatment/.

Jones, Antonio. 2023. "The Connection between Nutrition and Mental Health: What You Eat Matters." *Phat Muscle Society* (blog). May 1, 2023. https://www.phatmusclesociety.com/the-connection-between-nutrition-and-mental-health-what-you-eat-matters/.

Kabat-Zinn, J., L. Lipworth, and R. Burney. 1985. "The Clinical Use of Mindfulness Meditation for the Self-Regulation of Chronic Pain." *Journal of Behavioral Medicine* 8 (2): 163–90. https://doi.org/10.1007/BF00845519.

Kaur, Mandeep, Augustus Floyd, and Ana-Maria Balta. 2022. "Oppositional Defiant Disorder: Evidence-Based Review of Behavioral Treatment Programs." *Annals of*

Clinical Psychiatry: Official Journal of the American Academy of Clinical Psychiatrists 34 (1): 44–58. https://doi.org/10.12788/acp.0056.

Landon, Joel. 2024. "The Pursuit of More: How Less Can Lead to More Happiness." eQRP. January 3, 2024. https://eqrp.com/the-pursuit-of-more-how-less-can-lead-to-more-happiness/.

"Legal Rights." 2024. Project Pencil. 2024. https://projectpencil.com/legal-rights/.

Lynch, Britney. 2023. "The Impact of Folate on Anxiety: Unlocking Nature's Calming Nutrient." Regel Pharmalab. June 26, 2023. https://www.regelpharmalab.com/post/the-impact-of-folate-on-anxiety-unlocking-nature-s-calming-nutrient.

Morin, Amanda. n.d. "Nonverbal Signals: An Evidence-Based Behavior Strategy." Reading Rockets. https://www.readingrockets.org/topics/classroom-management/articles/nonverbal-signals-evidence-based-behavior-strategy.

Mousain-Bosc, M., Roche, M., Polge, A., Pradier, C., Rapin, J., and Bali, J. P. "Improvement of Neurobehavioral Disorders in Children Supplemented with Magnesium–Vitamin B6. II. Pervasive Developmental Disorder–Autism." *Magnesium Research* 19, no. 1 (2006): 53-62. https://doi.org/10.1684/mrh.2006.0007.

Muppalla, Sudheer Kumar, Sravya Vuppalapati, Apeksha Reddy Pulliahgaru, and Himabindu Sreenivasulu. n.d. "Effects of Excessive Screen Time on Child Development: An Updated Review and Strategies for Management." Cureus 15 (6): e40608. Accessed October 14, 2024. https://doi.org/10.7759/cureus.40608.

Neurolaunch. "Child Psychology and Color: Hues Influencing Young Minds." Accessed September 15, 2024. https://neurolaunch.com/child-psychology-color/.

"Nku Oppositional Defiant Disorder vs Conduct Disorder Comparative Essay Nursing Assignment Help." 2023. USA Prime Essays. September 2, 2023. https://usaprimeessays.com/nku-oppositional-defiant-disorder-vs-conduct-disorder-comparative-essay-nursing-assignment-help/.

"ODD: A Guide for Families." n.d. American Academy of Child and Adolescent Psychiatry. https://www.aacap.org/App_Themes/AACAP/docs/resource_centers/odd/odd_resource_center_odd_guide.pdf.

"Oppositional Defiant Disorder." n.d. American Association for Marriage and Family Therapy. https://www.aamft.org/AAMFT/Consumer_Updates/Oppositional_Defiant_Disorder.aspx.

"Oppositional Defiant Disorder (Odd) - Symptoms and Causes." n.d. Mayo Clinic. https://www.mayoclinic.org/diseases-conditions/oppositional-defiant-disorder/symptoms-causes/syc-20375831.

"Oppositional Defiant Disorder (Odd): Children and Pre-Teens." n.d. Raising Children Network. https://raisingchildren.net.au/school-age/health-daily-care/school-age-mental-health-concerns/odd.

"Oppositional Defiant Disorder (ODD) in Children." n.d. Cedars-Sinai. https://www.

cedars-sinai.org/health-library/diseases-and-conditions---pediatrics/o/oppositional-defiant-disorder-odd-in-children.html.

"Oppositional Defiant Disorder Resource Center." 2019. American Academy of Child & Adolescent Psychiatry. June 2019. https://www.aacap.org/AACAP/Families_and_Youth/Resource_Centers/Oppositional_Defiant_Disorder_Resource_Center/Home.aspx.

"Oppositional Defiant Disorder Strategies: 8 Discipline Rules." 2018. *ADDitude* (blog). April 27, 2018. https://www.additudemag.com/oppositional-defiant-disorder-discipline-rules-video/.

"Oppositional (ODD)." n.d. Luna Learning Center. https://www.lunarespiteandlearning.com/fosteringspecialneeds/categories/oppostional-odd.

Poppendieck, Donna. 2023. "Herbs for Your Health: Harnessing Nature's Healing Power." *Health and Wellness Online* (blog). August 3, 2023. https://healthandwellnessonline.org/herbs-your-health-harnessing-natures/.

Raine, Adrian, Jill Portnoy, Jianghong Liu, Tashneem Mahoomed, and Joseph Hibbeln. 2015. "Reduction in Behavior Problems with Omega-3 Supplementation in Children Aged 8-16 Years: A Randomized, Double-Blind, Placebo-Controlled, Stratified, Parallel-Grouptrial." *Journal of Child Psychology and Psychiatry, and Allied Disciplines* 56 (5): 509–20. https://doi.org/10.1111/jcpp.12314.

Robinson, Dr Stacey. 2018. "Benefits of Functional Medicine." *Robinson MD* (blog). November 7, 2018. https://robinsonmed.com/benefits-of-functional-medicine/.

"Screen Time and Depression in Kids and Adolescents." n.d. Gryphon. https://gryphonconnect.com/blogs/gryphon/screen-time-and-depression-in-kids-and-adolescents.

"Simple Tips to Maintain a Healthy Lifestyle in a Busy World." n.d. *Quarry Knowledge* (blog). http://www.valleysend.co.za/Dec_18_733/index.html.

Sounders, Beata. 2019. "Positive Reinforcement for Kids: 11+ Examples for Parents." PositivePsychology.Com. April 9, 2019. https://positivepsychology.com/parenting-positive-reinforcement/.

Strøm, Vegard, Marita S Fønhus, Eilin Ekeland, and Gro Jamtvedt. 2017. "Physical Exercise for Oppositional Defiant Disorder and Conduct Disorder in Children and Adolescents." *The Cochrane Database of Systematic Reviews* 2017 (1): CD010670. https://doi.org/10.1002/14651858.CD010670.pub2.

"Strong Parent Communication in Special Education." 2022. Full Speed Ahead (blog). January 24, 2022. https://www.fullspedahead.com/parent-communication-in-special-education/.

"Tablet Use among Children Associated with Increased Anger, Frustration." 2024. Contemporary Pediatrics. August 13, 2024. https://www.contemporarypediatrics.com/view/tablet-use-among-children-associated-with-increased-anger-frustration.

Thalheimer, Edward. 2023. "Navigating Behavior Challenges at School." Dr. Edward

Thalheimer Education & Tutoring. August 21, 2023. https://dredwardthalheimer.co/navigating-behavior-challenges-at-school/.

"The Positive Impact of Exercise on Mental Health." 2023. June 15, 2023. https://www.healthbenefitstimes.com/the-positive-impact-of-exercise-on-mental-health/.

Thomas, Jody. n.d. "How to Have Difficult Conversations with Kids." Meg Foundation (blog). https://www.megfoundationforpain.org/articles/tips-for-tough-conversations-with-kids/.

"Unlocking the Potential of the Mind: The Best Focus Supplements for Cognitive Enhancement." 2023. Big Sky Reviews. December 8, 2023. https://www.bigskyreviews.com/best-focus-supplements/.

Vaher, Kadi, Debby Bogaert, Hilary Richardson, and James P Boardman. 2022. "Microbiome-Gut-Brain Axis in Brain Development, Cognition and Behavior during Infancy and Early Childhood." *Developmental Review* 66 (December):101038. https://doi.org/10.1016/j.dr.2022.101038.

Villamor, Eduardo, Sonia Robinson, Constanza Marín, Henry Oliveros, Mercedes Mora-Plazas, and Betsy Lozoff. "Vitamin D Deficiency in Middle Childhood Is Related to Behavior Problems in Adolescence." *The Journal of Nutrition* (2019). https://doi.org/10.1093/jn/nxz185.

Vyas, Chinmay, et al. "Supplementation with B Vitamins Improves Mood and Cognitive Function in Children: Implications for Managing Oppositional Defiant Disorder Symptoms." *American Journal of Clinical Nutrition* 119, no. 2 (2024): 345-356. https://doi.org/10.1093/ajcn/nqaa345.

"What Is Holistic Parenting?" 2023. *San Antonio Moms* (blog). June 13, 2023. https://sanantoniomomblogs.com/what-is-holistic-parenting/.

"What is the Purpose of Digital Life? A Comprehensive Guide to Understanding Our Connected World – Exploring Infinite Innovations in the Digital World." February 12, 2024. https://www.mustardseed.co.jp/what-is-the-purpose-of-digital-life-a-comprehensive-guide-to-understanding-our-connected-world/

Wilde, Kendra. 2021. "Six Ways to Deal with Parental Burnout." Greater Good Magazine. September 3, 2021. https://greatergood.berkeley.edu/article/item/six_ways_to_deal_with_parental_burnout.

Yoon, Susan, Jennifer L. Bellamy, Wonhee Kim, and Dalhee Yoon. 2018. "Father Involvement and Behavior Problems among Preadolescents at Risk of Maltreatment." *Journal of Child and Family Studies* 27 (2): 494–504. https://www.ncbi.nlm.nih.gov/pmc/articles/PMC5826550/.

Made in the USA
Monee, IL
26 April 2025